these

are

the

waterfalls

in

my

head

JeFF Stumpo

Yas Press
University of New Hampshire
English Department
230 Hamilton Smith Hall
Durham, NH 03824
Managing Editor: Danielle Jones

Published in partnership with Pink Eraser Press
Cover design: Ashley Halsey and JeFF Stumpo
Interior design: Ashley Halsey
Managing editor: Molly McGrath

Printed in the USA

"A majority of recurrent dreams experienced during adulthood are described as being negatively toned and questionnaire studies of adults' retrospective accounts of recurrent dreams experienced during child-hood show that almost 90% are described as being unpleasant or of a threatening nature."

– Gauchat, et al.

introduction

When I first read JeFF Stumpo's *these are the waterfalls in my head*, I was struck by how insistently the book returns us to a single word: *tonight*. Each poem begins there, in the immediate, unsettled present, a space that feels intimate and inescapable. This repetition isn't decorative, rather deliberate. It is the book's ethical stance. These poems insist that what happens in the mind, the body, memory, and dream is happening now.

Again and again, the poems open with an address that refuses distance: "[Tonight you are washing your hands in the bathroom sink...]," "[Tonight you are hungry and faithless in a cathedral...]," "[Tonight you are not the sailor but the shipwreck...]" From the first pages, the reader is implicated. The second person does not offer escape. You are not observing these scenes; you are inside them. Bodies shift. Speakers change. As readers, we become each of these speakers. We are witnesses, participants, and, at times, complicit. The poems do not allow us to stand outside violence, fear, or power. They ask us to recognize how entangled we are.

These poems intrigued me further once I learned their origin story. They grew not only from the poet's own dreams, but from conversations, from listening, from the dreams and fears of others. As the book unfolds, it becomes clear that *these are the waterfalls in my head* is a collective experience rendered through lyric imagination. The nightmares belong to no one person. They echo. They recur. They are shared. This is a book shaped by permission, by the careful and charged act of writing from and alongside the lived experiences of others.

This expansiveness feels Whitmanian to me. Stumpo's imagination is capacious, yet it is not appropriative. The poems do not claim ownership over others' suffering; they honor it. They listen. They take on the ethical risk of speaking across difference with care and accountability. It's my belief that white men should write about uncomfortable truths, including race, as an acknowledgment of shared history and shared responsibility. Silence is not neutrality. This book understands that and moves toward the uncomfortable deliberately.

Reading this collection, I was reminded of *Crush* by Richard Siken, a book that famously unsettled readers when it first appeared. Louise Glück described *Crush* precisely when she called it "a book about panic." I felt a similar panic here—panic as urgency, as a refusal of safety. The poems keep opening into new scenarios, new dangers, new moral positions. Each "[Tonight you are...]" multiplies into possibility. I found myself needing to know more. They haunted me. They followed me into sleep.

And even in sleep, this book insists, we do not escape reality. War, loss, grief, surveillance, ecological collapse—these forces remain present on the dreaming body. In one poem, "the news is a screaming hydra"; in another, "Death's Own Metronome" keeps time as the speaker fails again and again to save what they love. And perhaps most unsettling of all, even joy arrives under threat. Wonder flickers briefly—whales migrating through the sky, blueberries rolling into open palms—only to remind us how fragile those moments are, how quickly they can vanish.

I chose JeFF Stumpo's *these are the waterfalls in my head* for its inventive formal risk and its unflinching message. This is a book that refuses rest.

It asks readers to remain present to fear, empathy, and the uneasy recognition that our inner lives are shaped by one another. It is a book that believes attention itself is an ethical act. And poetry is the engine for that attention.

Diannely Antigua
UNH Nossrat Yassini Poet in Residence
Judge of the 2026 Granite State Poetry Prize

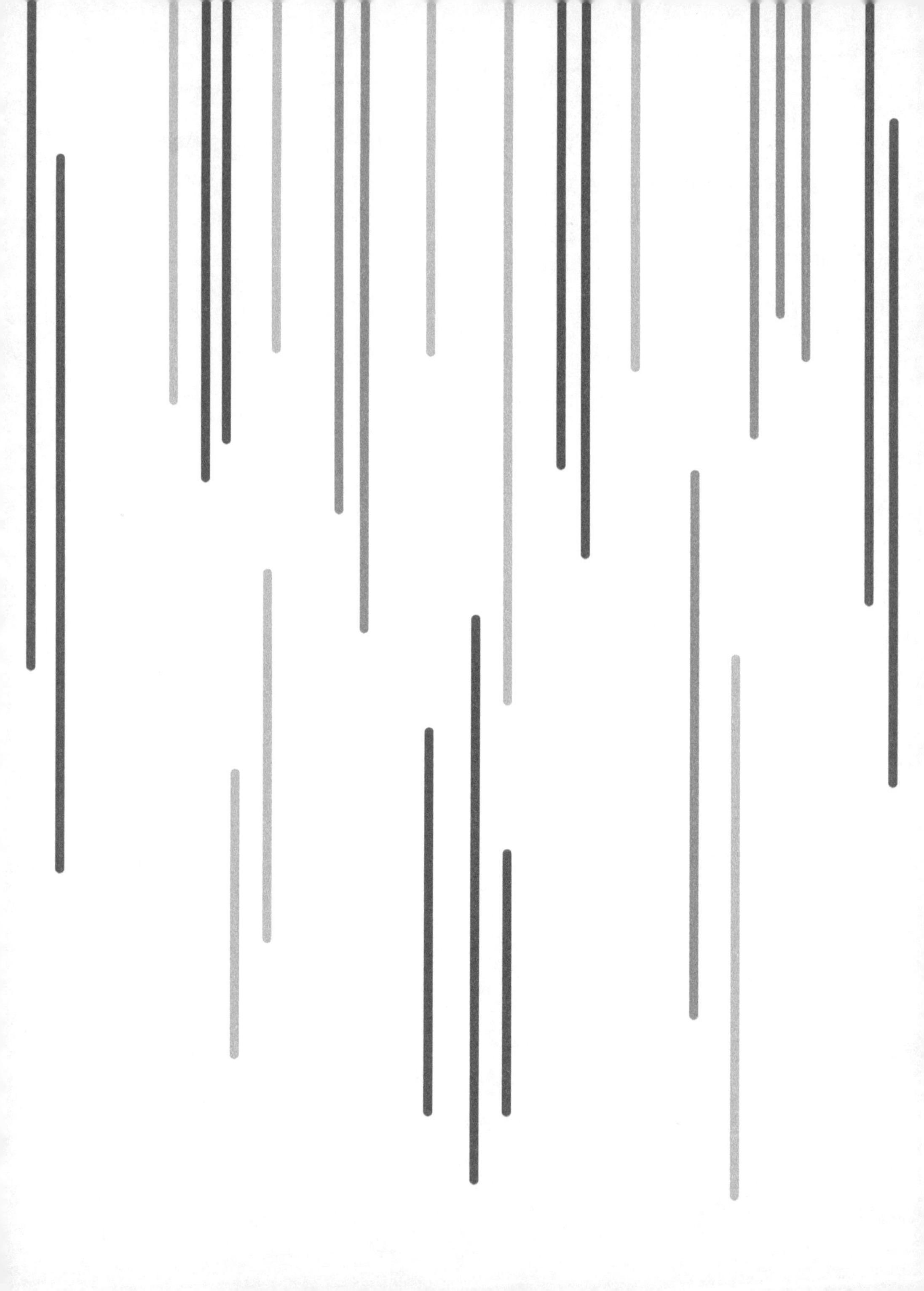

contents

Tonight you are washing your hands in the bathroom sink when your reflection reaches out and grabs you by the wrist. You stumble back so that you can't be pulled into the mirror, but that's not its goal. *It* wants *out*. It's crouching on its sink, slinking through the space where the mirror was. You see its home and wish you hadn't. There are dead vines extending into your world, blood flowers blooming dustily. Everything is covered in thorns, even the you that wants you gone. You are trying to wake up, but you've always known you were the most frightening thing in your life.

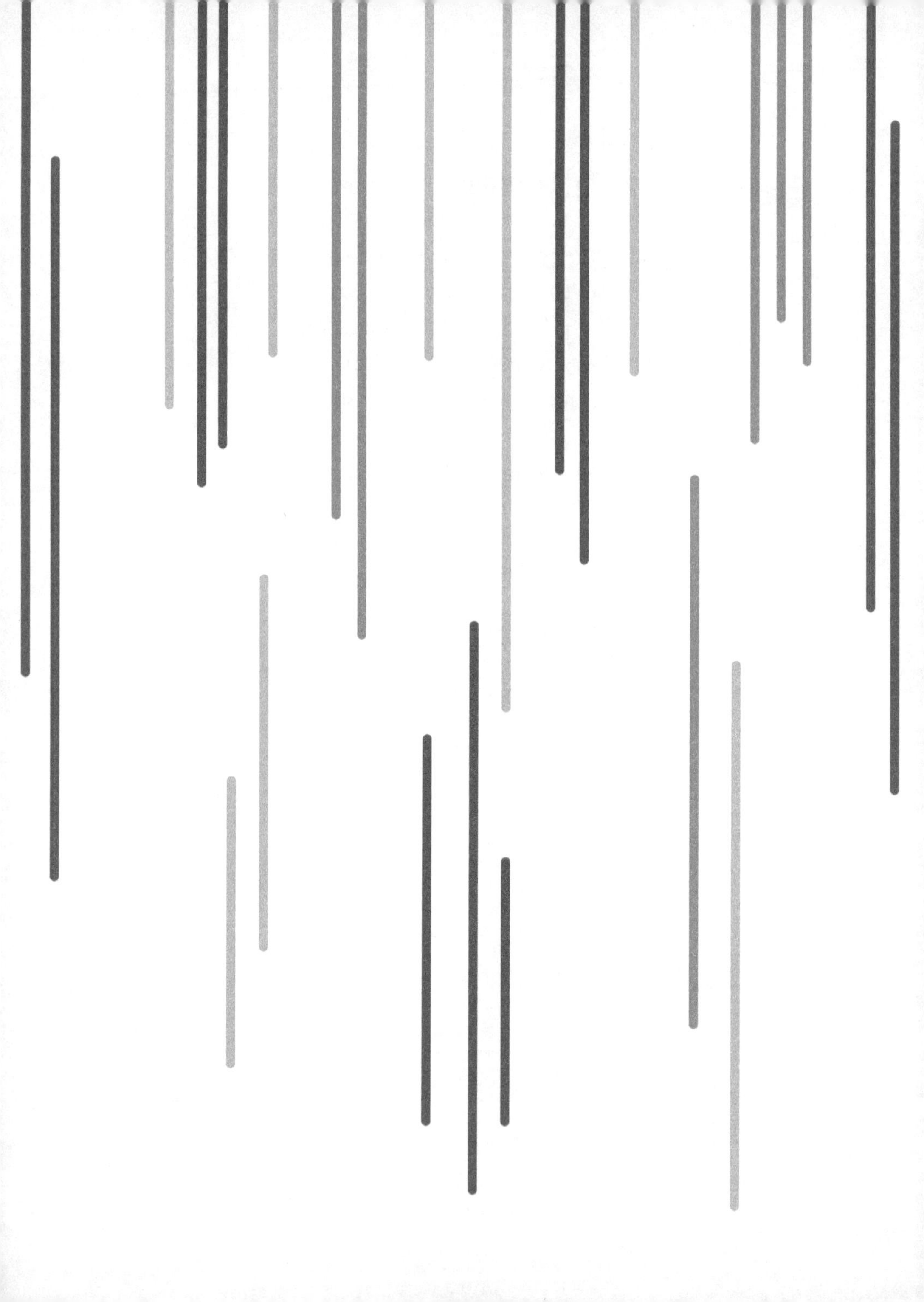

Tonight you are looking at a beautiful woman, when a hand holds up a lighter to the side of her head and lights her hair on fire. You can't look away, and she can't move. You are watching her burn to death, and the whole of your world is flame and wax that you know isn't wax. Every time you start to wonder if this is a metaphor, she screams, so you stop looking for meaning. You are watching her die, and you promise yourself you won't look in the mirror when you wake. You might be a beautiful woman. You might be a hand.

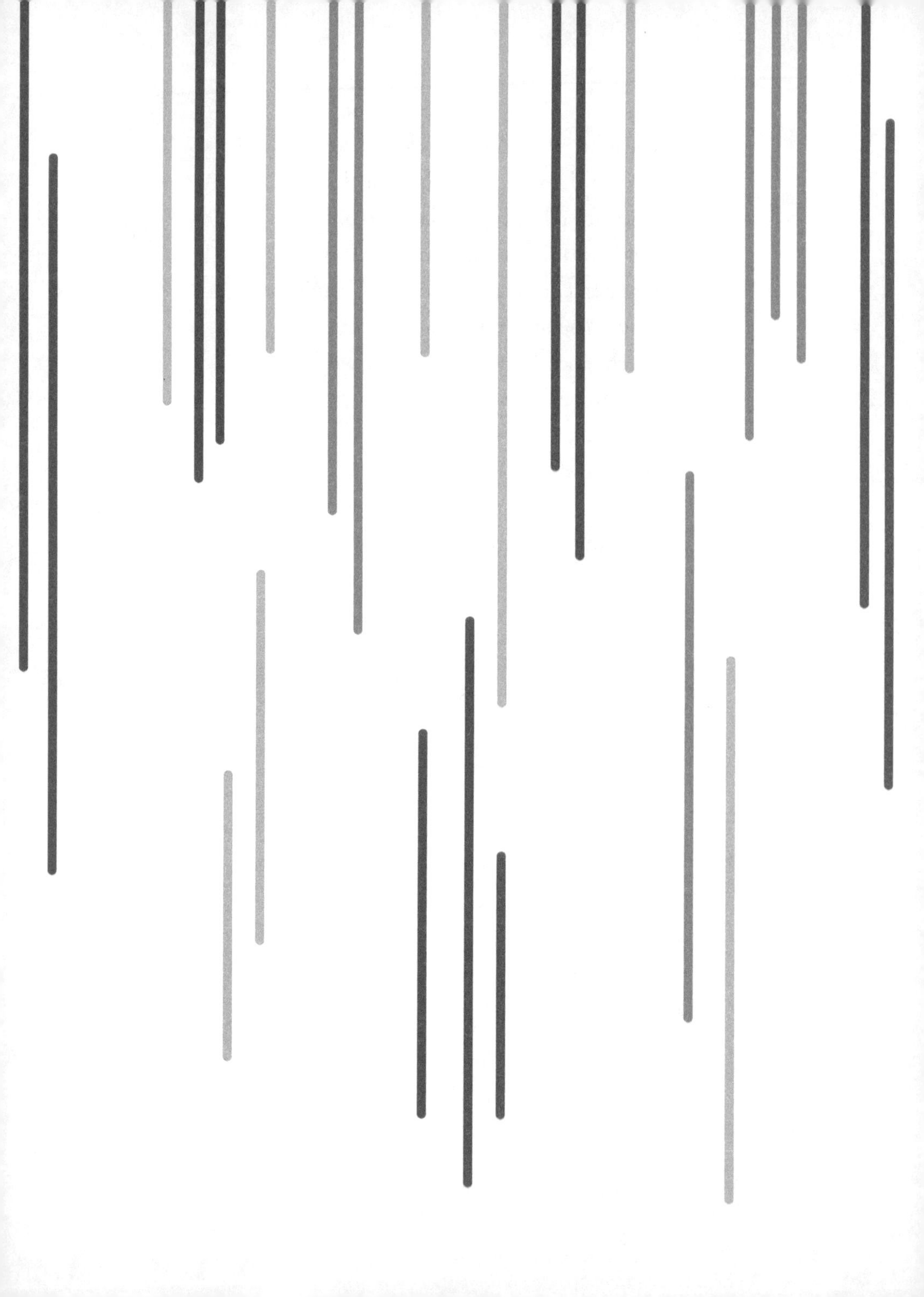

Tonight you are on a dark backroad, your headlights the only sign of civilization. You pass signs you can't read. The road never curves, yet you can't see more than a few yards ahead. Before you know it, you've been pulled over, the red and blue flashes destroying the sanctity of your mirrors. A deer walks up to your window on its hind legs, knocks with a hoof. You're trying to explain that you haven't done anything, when its face splits open and the skull drips blood as it orders you to get out. There is a deer in your back seat staring at you with empty eye sockets. There is a pain in your heart like an antler. You're not going to make it home. You're as good as a skull on a wall.

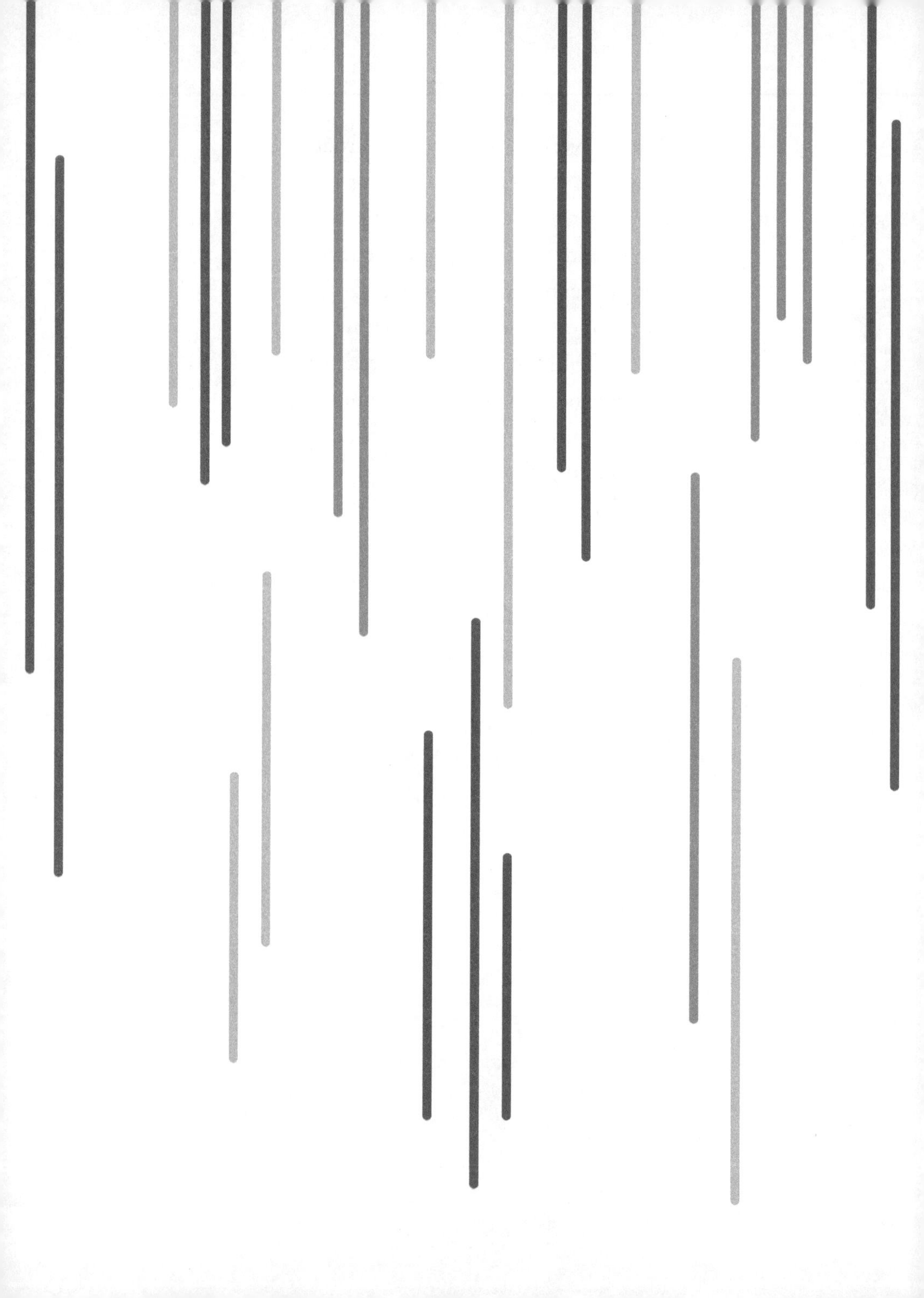

Tonight you are an insect bound by window-magic, tracing the rectangle six feet at a time, enraptured by light and trapped by glass, cognizant only that you need to escape, not how, an obsession, the idea beating in your mind like your carapace against the pane, sure that you should be smarter than this with no concept of what that smarter feels like, a thought hitting you like a hand, that you have so many eyes but can't see your way out, a conviction taking flight, maybe this time around, maybe this time things will be different.

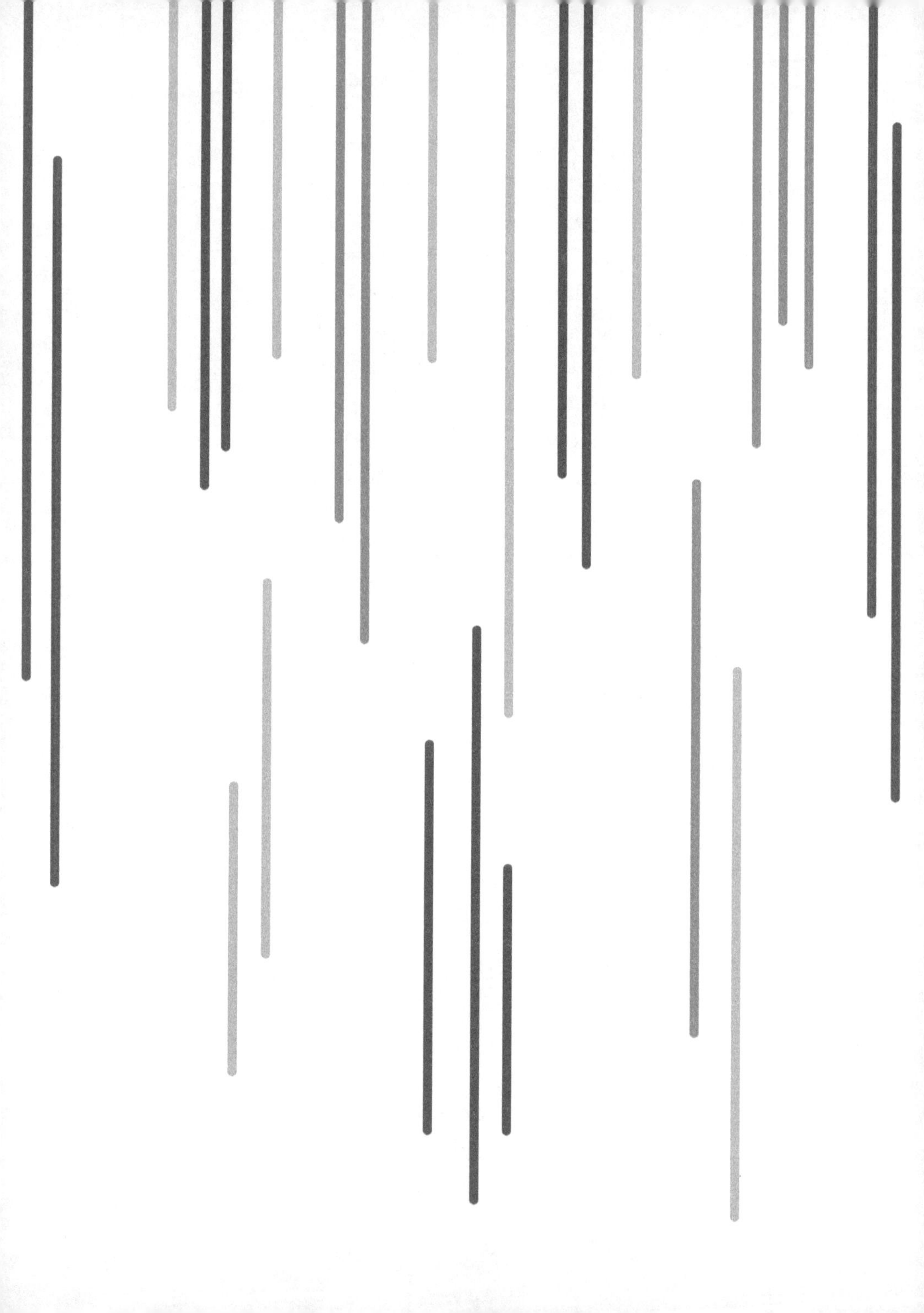

Tonight you are pregnant and your fetus has a gun. It is lazily waving inside your swollen belly. It is threatening your spinal cord, your organs. Your fetus can't even think, yet you are humming lullabies like your life depends on them. Your life depends on them. You are in a yard in front of a nondescript house, shoving a rake impossibly inside you. Police are approaching with their guns drawn. You point to the gun lying in a pool of fetus. Don't they see it. Don't they know what would have happened. The police are shouting things you can't hear over the feedback, like cicadas have taken up in your brain. You feel your uterus swell again. You grow to the size of the world. There is an atom bomb inside you. You never wanted this. You never wished for a weapon.

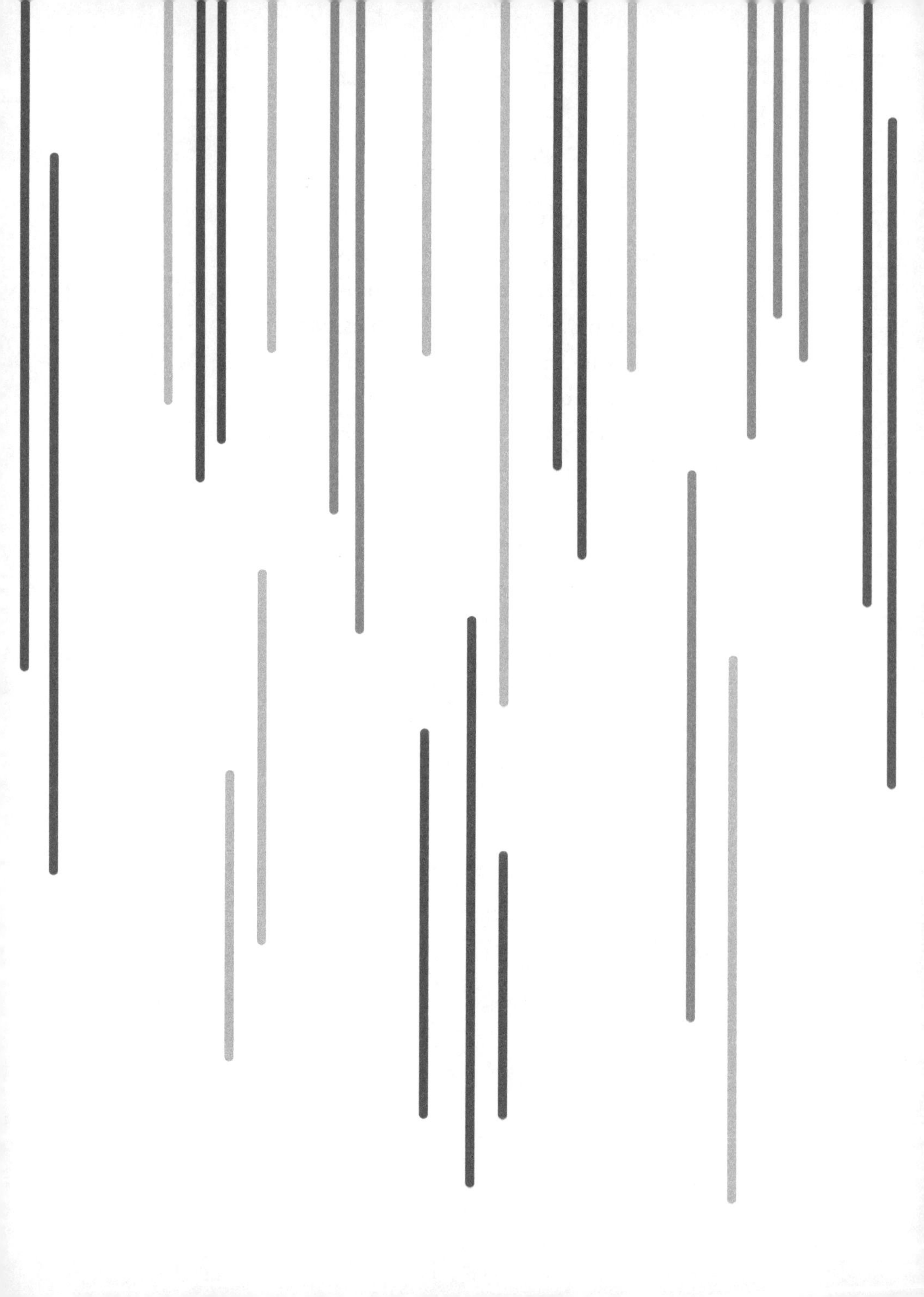

Tonight you are the echo in the bottom of the well. Tonight you are the echo in the bottom of the well and the plucked string. Tonight you are the echo in the bottom of the well and the plucked string and the bursting bubble. Tonight you are the echo in the bottom of the well and the plucked string and the bursting bubble and the spheres gliding in the hands of the juggler. Tonight you are a bubble plucked safely from a well, the music of the spheres, Echo calling, starburst and algae bloom, abiogenesis, a single cell clinging to a deep sea vent, a promise at the bottom of the ocean.

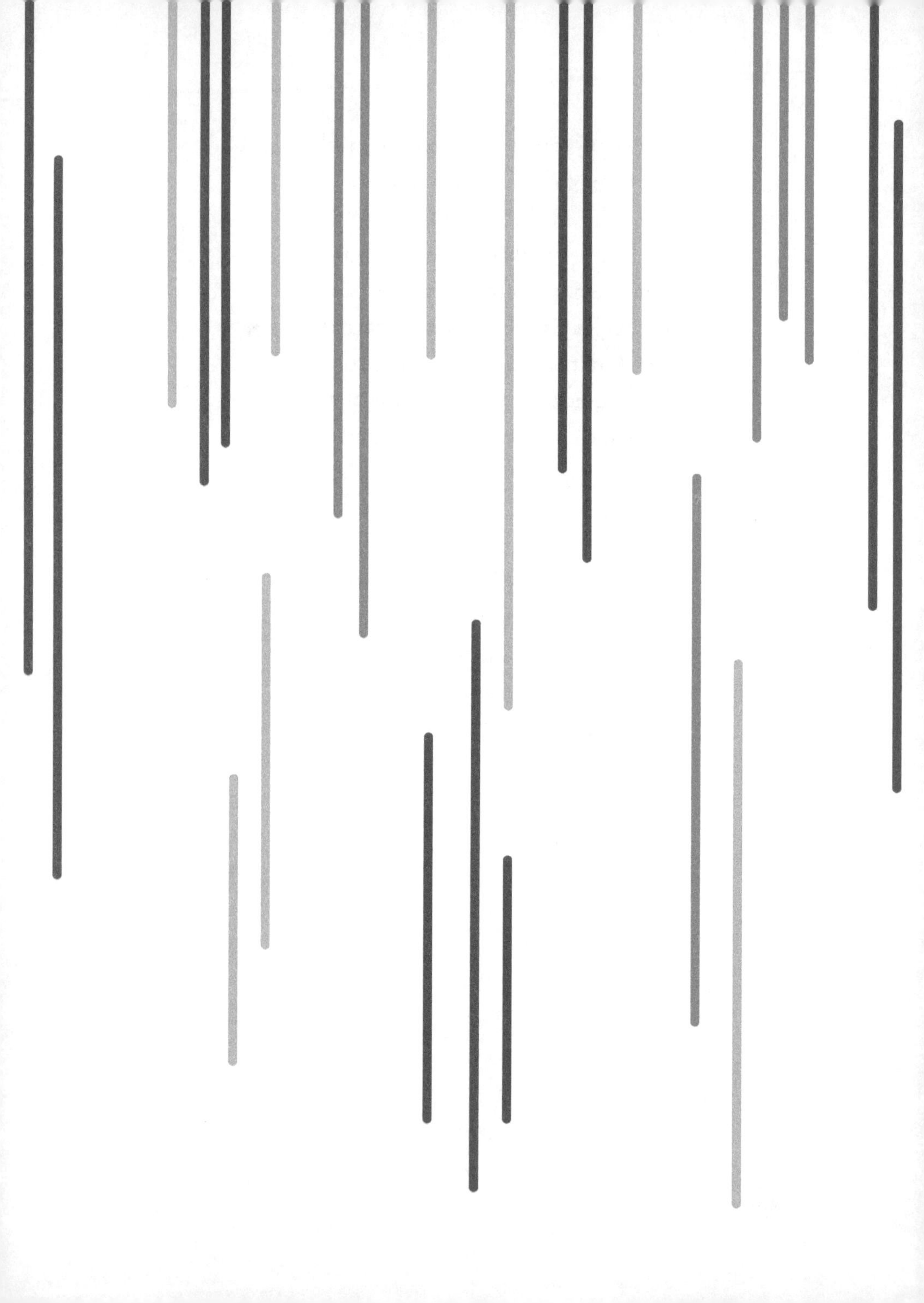

Tonight you are the means and the ends. You are the bullet riding the firestorm. You are Valkyrie, reaper, third rail. You are centuries of propaganda stuffed into eighteen years. You are some small town's exit wound. You are the hand given permission to pull the switch and the switch and the electric revelation. You are Revelation. You are the Bible pages strewn across the highway, the hotel unbound from Earth, the tornado lifting up into the sky as though its work here were done.

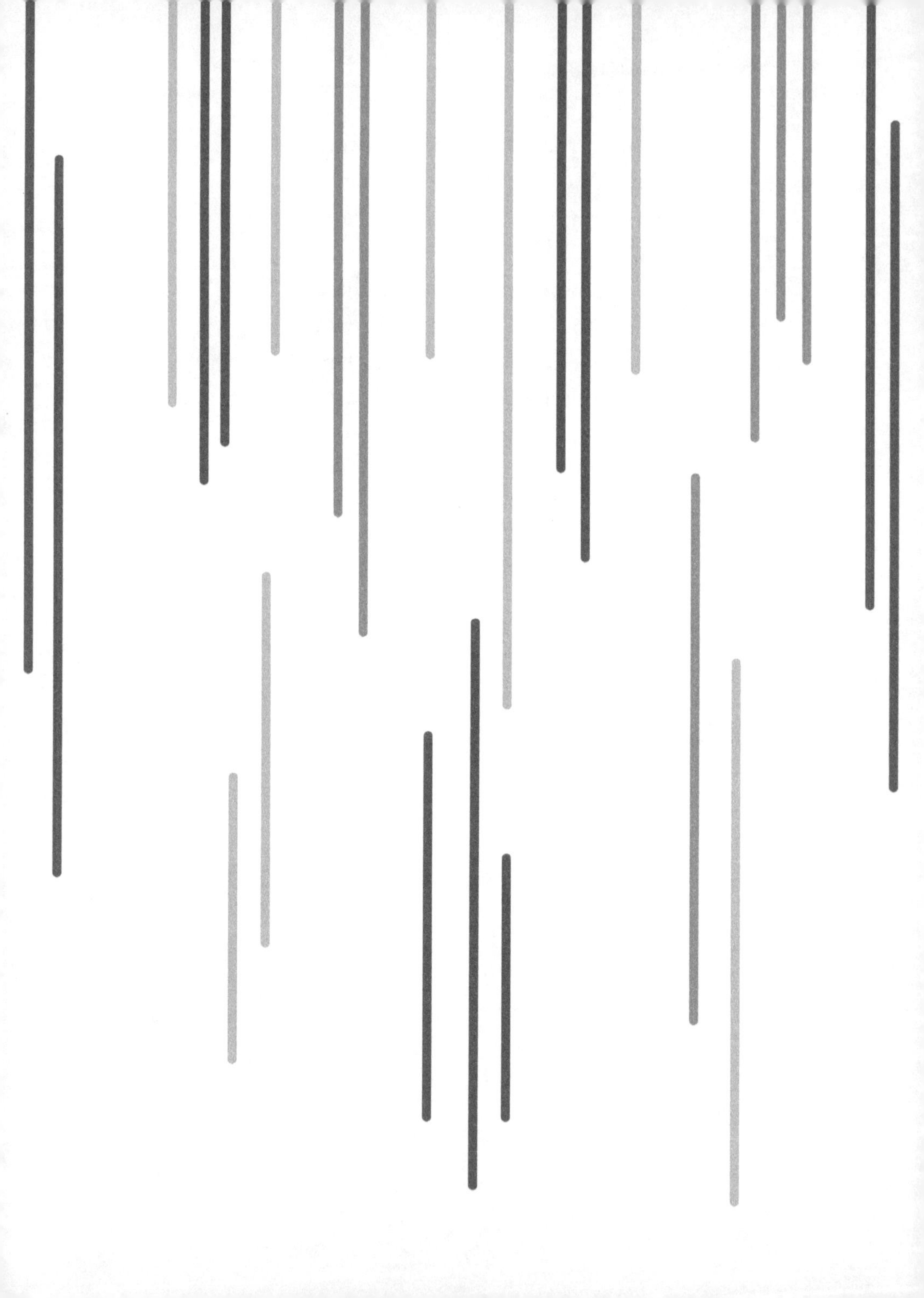

Tonight you are at Times Square or possibly the end of the world. The streets are filled with turtles, uniform of mind, crawling block by block like Fate. The buildings around you disappear. Appear. Disappear. Appear. You are being carried somewhere on the backs of the turtles. You try to scramble free but are helpless as an upturned shell. You reach for a traffic light and it phases through your hand. Ahead, the street has cracked open and turtles are spilling over the edge. You remember that lemmings don't really kill themselves but the knowledge doesn't matter. The crack in the street is eating skyscrapers, detritus. You lurch forward and fall. Earth is calling in her little ones, *Come home, come home.*

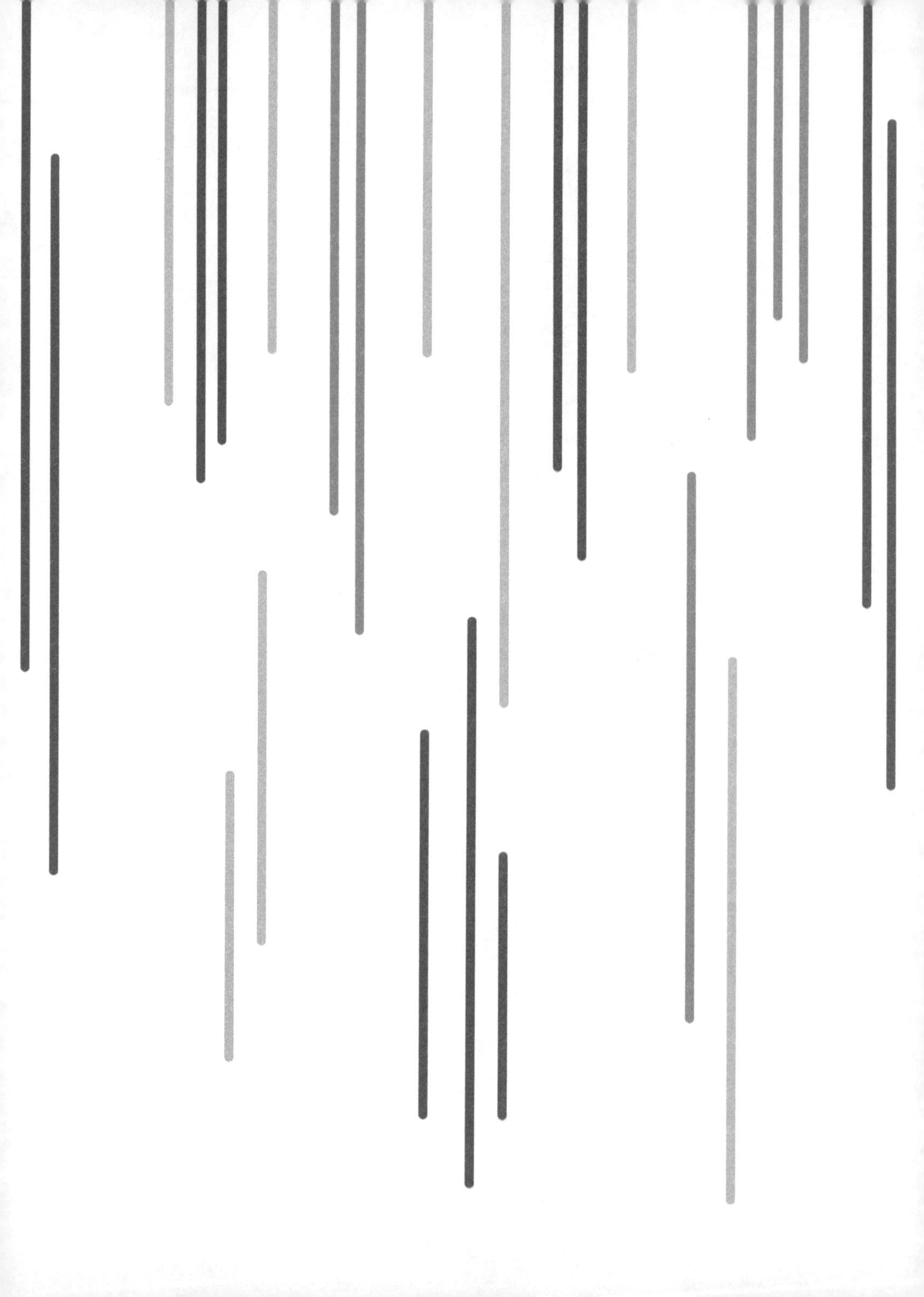

Tonight you are peddling your skeleton outside Prague, your skin hanging off the handles of a pushcart. When the wind blows in your ears, it pushes the word *gold* out of your mouth and sends your soul rattling about the sacks you call lungs. You don't remember coming here, just the need for coin. A child who is neither a girl nor a boy skips up to you. *Gold*, the wind whistles out of you. But the child giggles and calls you *Silly. You can't walk home with bones of gold.* And like that, they are threading you back together, a doll that lost its stuffing. Like that, they are sending you on your way.

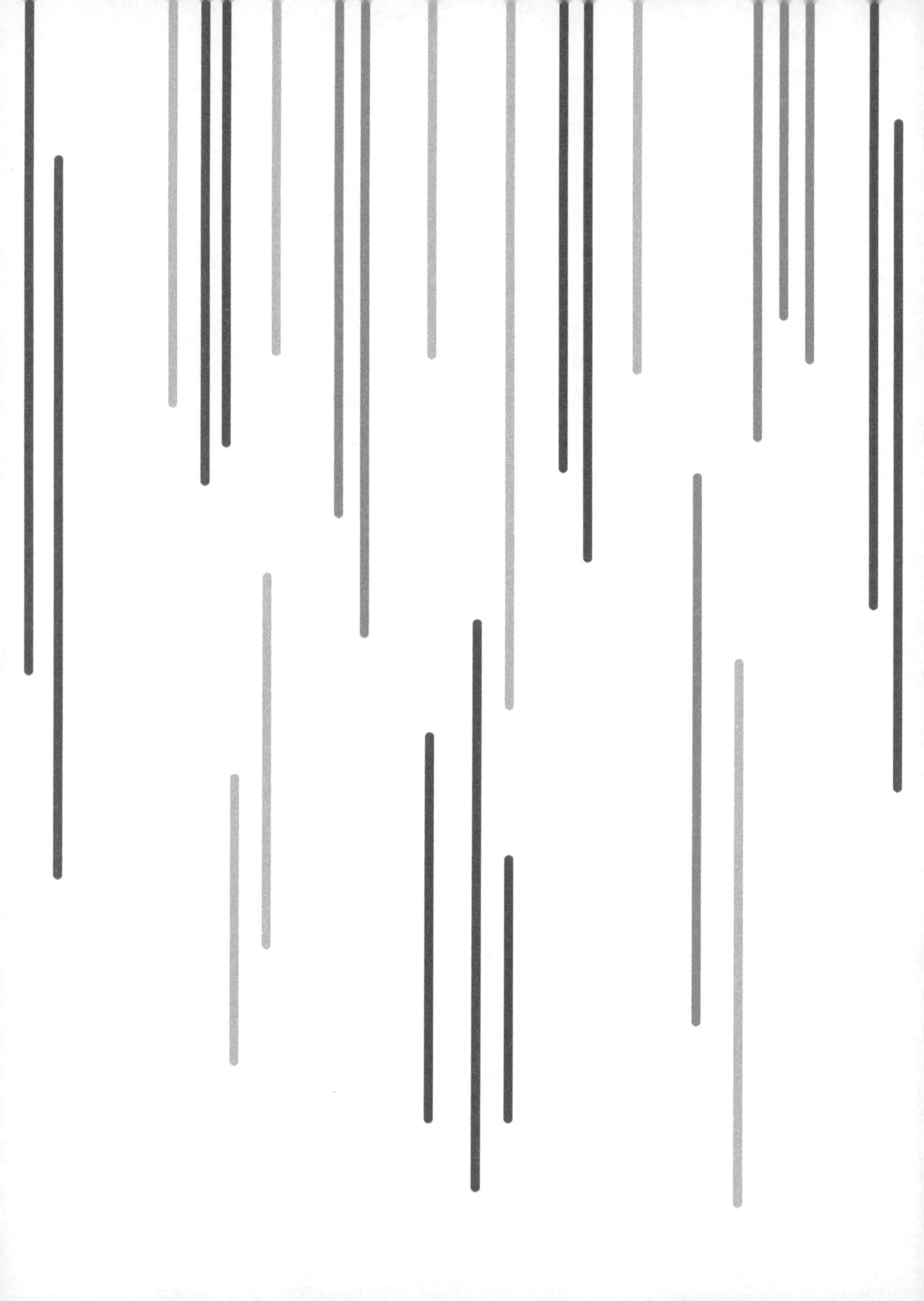

Tonight you lie on your own couch, trying to head off fixation. Your cigar is just a. You hold it oscillating between Cuban and. You are not. You tell yourself this. You flip through your notebook, and it is filled with pictures of you riding the night. The cigar is in your fingers, which place it to your lips. You take a luxurious puff. *Wake up*, you whimper, and linger, eyes glazing. *Up*, you manage. *Up*. The notebook falls from your other hand. *Gravity is repression*, you think and try to not. You know how you will feel when you awaken. You can already feel the cold sweat coming.

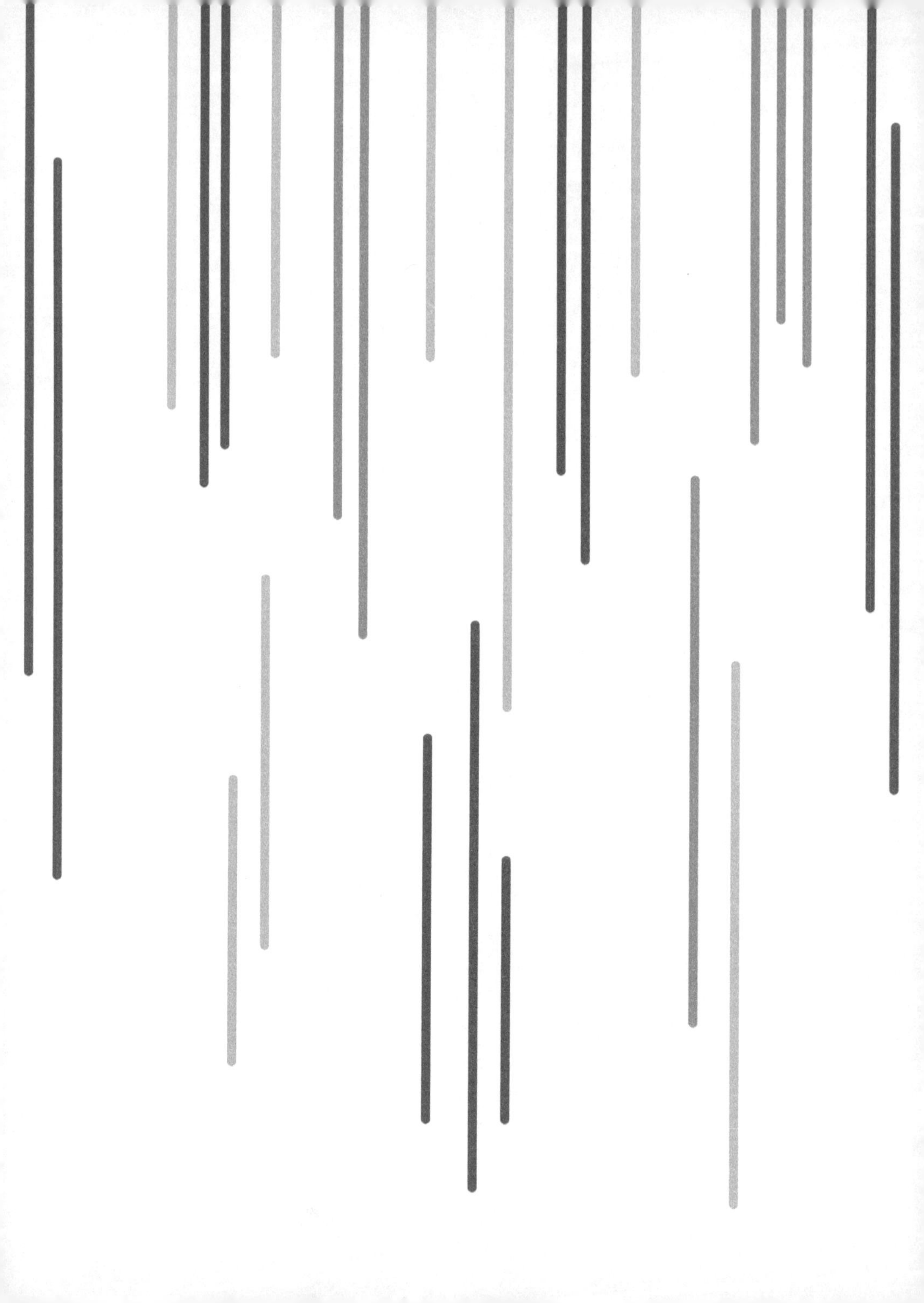

Tonight you are having The Talk with your son, but you can't see his face. Your son has no face. Your voice is muffled. You're not sure you're getting through. He doesn't nod or reply, and you have to tell him this. He has to know this. You're getting angry. You shout like there's a hand on your mouth. You scream and choke on your own livid orders. You are so angry, and he has no face. You are furiously trying to keep your boy alive when it hits you. You're looking at him like a cop. You're looking at him like a coroner. Your sweet baby boy, your whole world, nothing more.

Tonight you can't find the source of the drums. You're in a room that you think is your bedroom, and the drums beat in your ears no matter where you stand. You're in a town square in New England. You're on a street corner in LA. You're at the Alamo. Always the drumbeats in your ears. You cover them, try to mumble another tune. It sounds like Yankee Doodle dying. Snatches of something you once read flash in time with the rhythm. A country built on sacred burial grounds. There are mushrooms growing out of your back, and you are trying to tear up the floorboards of a gallows with broken fingernails. You stare through the noose like a telescope. Someone said you can find a city on a hill through it, but all you can see up there is a stone table where your forefathers cut out a thousand beating hearts.

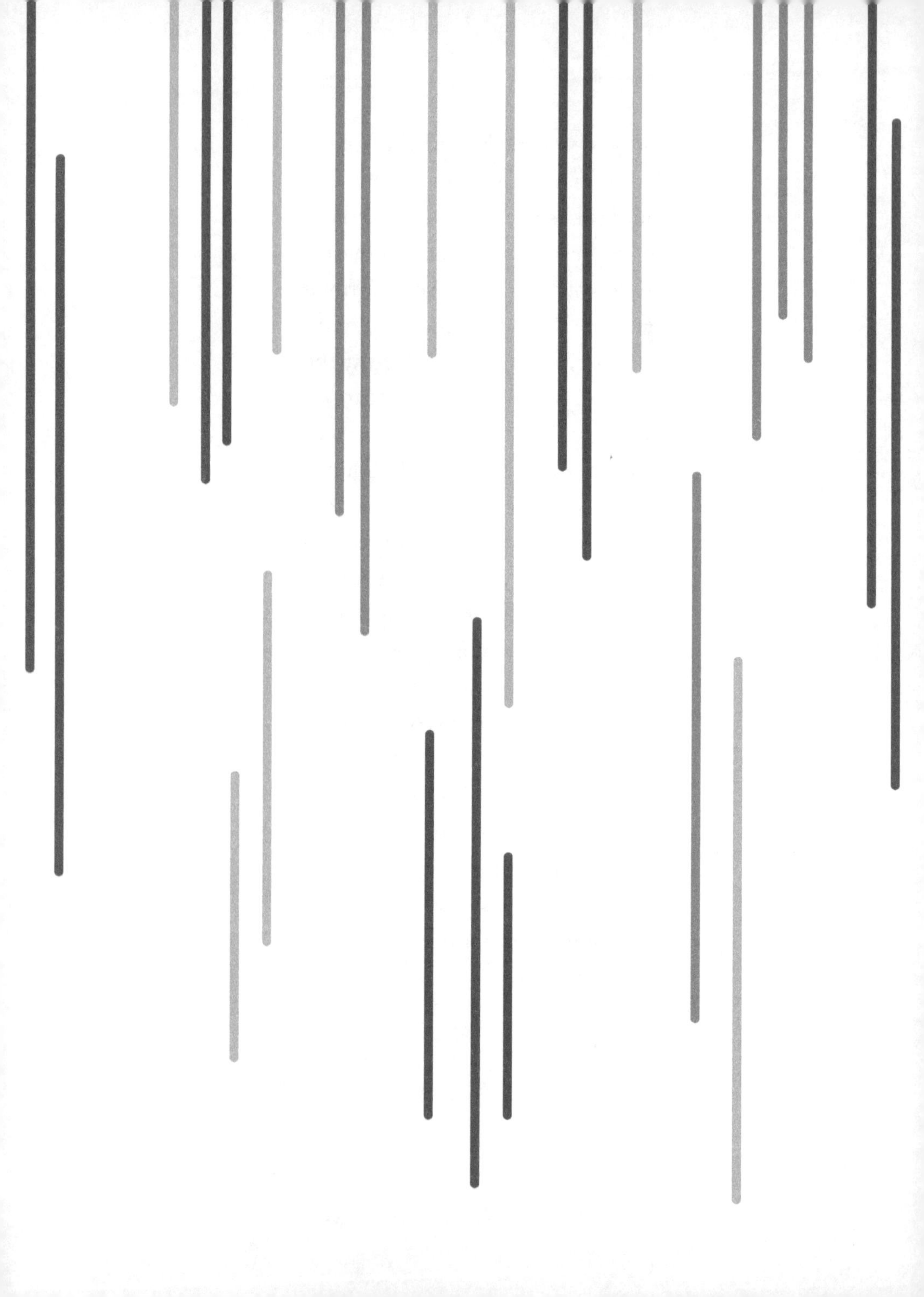

Tonight you are hungry and faithless in a cathedral. To say it is crowded is an understatement. Starving people lie atop one another, stacks on stacks on stacks on stacks. The children are crying. Everyone is in rags except the priests, who are not there at all. You rattle the locked doors, and it sounds like a thousand stomachs rumbling. The adults are weeping, too, now, and the children are trying to drink their tears, but everything evaporates too soon. You know it's wrong, but you keep thinking ten percent of the human body is water. You grip the busts of saints, try to crush them into bread. You are overturning basins that hold no holy liquids. You have a hammer with which you smash columns to bits, cast them before the people who break their teeth on them. In your head, the old parable echoes, *you can't squeeze blood from a stone.*

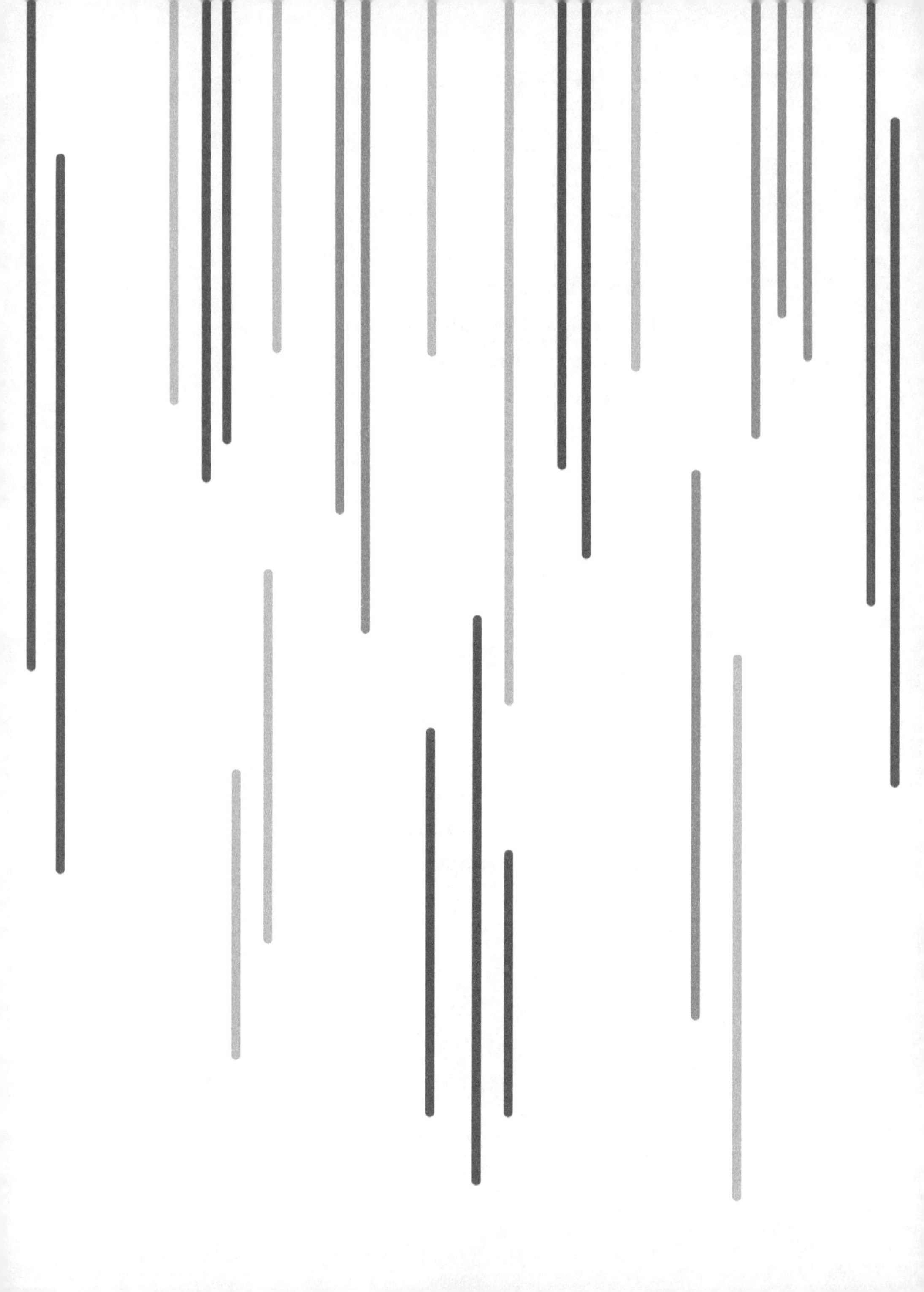

Tonight you are scraping the floor of a subway station with your tongue as though approaching an emperor's throne. All of you, the gritty and grimy, licking inch by filthy inch toward the turnstiles. It might be a race. You can't be sure of that, just that you can't lift face from concrete or else an unseen boot cracks down on your skull. From time to time, out of the corner of your eye, you see a head smack flat, a face come up bloodied. The invisible police keep you moving. The floor is thick with detritus. You feel a coiling in your gut and eject your whole stomach like a frog. The boot you can't see crushes it as you try to wipe off the rotten food and the caked dirt. You are stuffing it back into your mouth as quickly as you can. You don't want to know what they'll do if you don't apologize quickly.

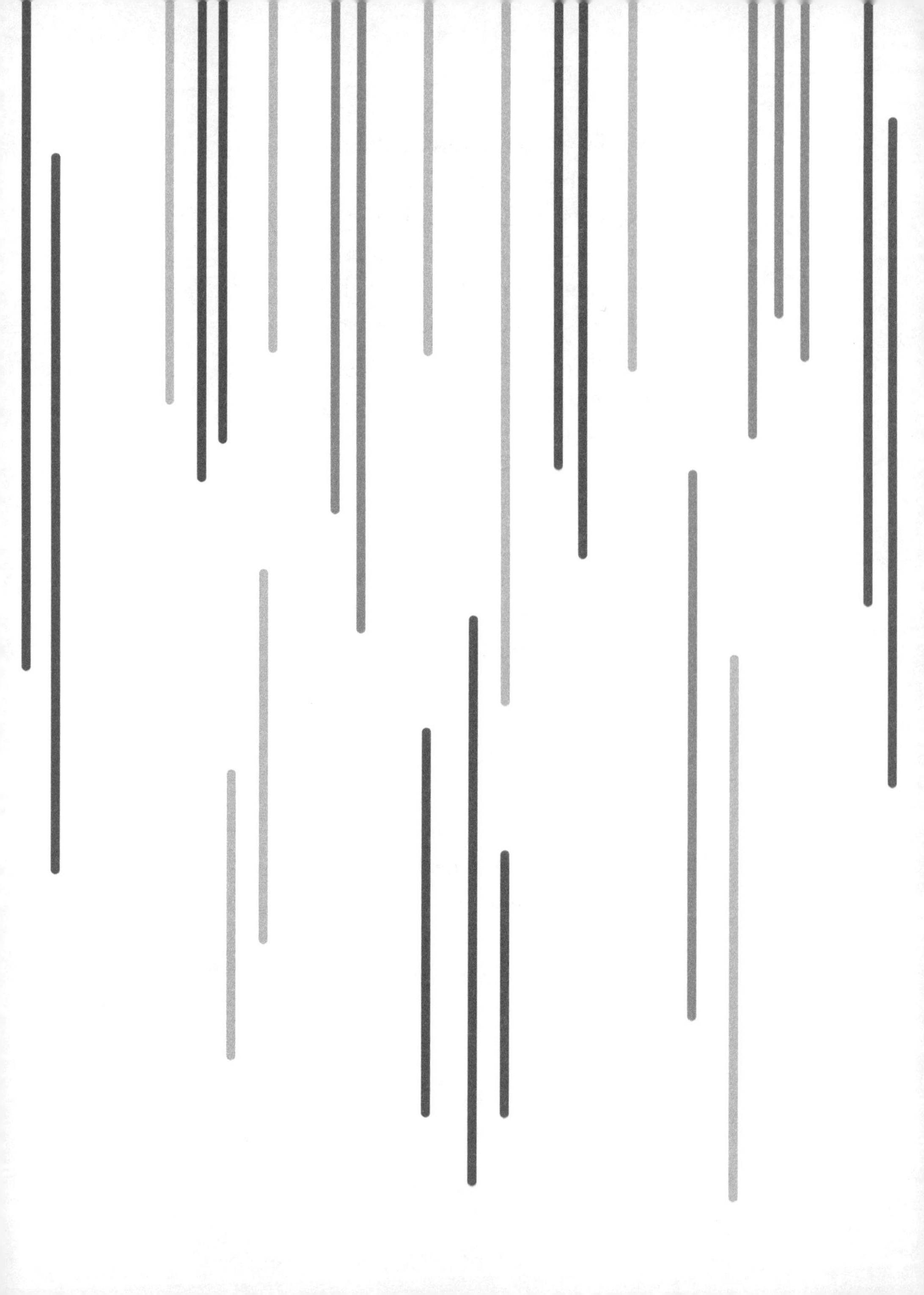

Tonight you are caught in a strobe-light childhood. Your dad, drunk and lurching and fisticuffs incarnate. The creek and the cloud of biting bugs. The roadside dog carcass you once called friend. The barn, darkened by thunderclouds, and its sharp metal music. The edge of town and the waiting clique. The homeless man in the alley and the thing he asked you to do. Years pass and scatter like lightning-scared horses. *Who left the door open?* asks the owl outside your bedroom. Who do you think you are that a highway built by men could take you away from that place forever.

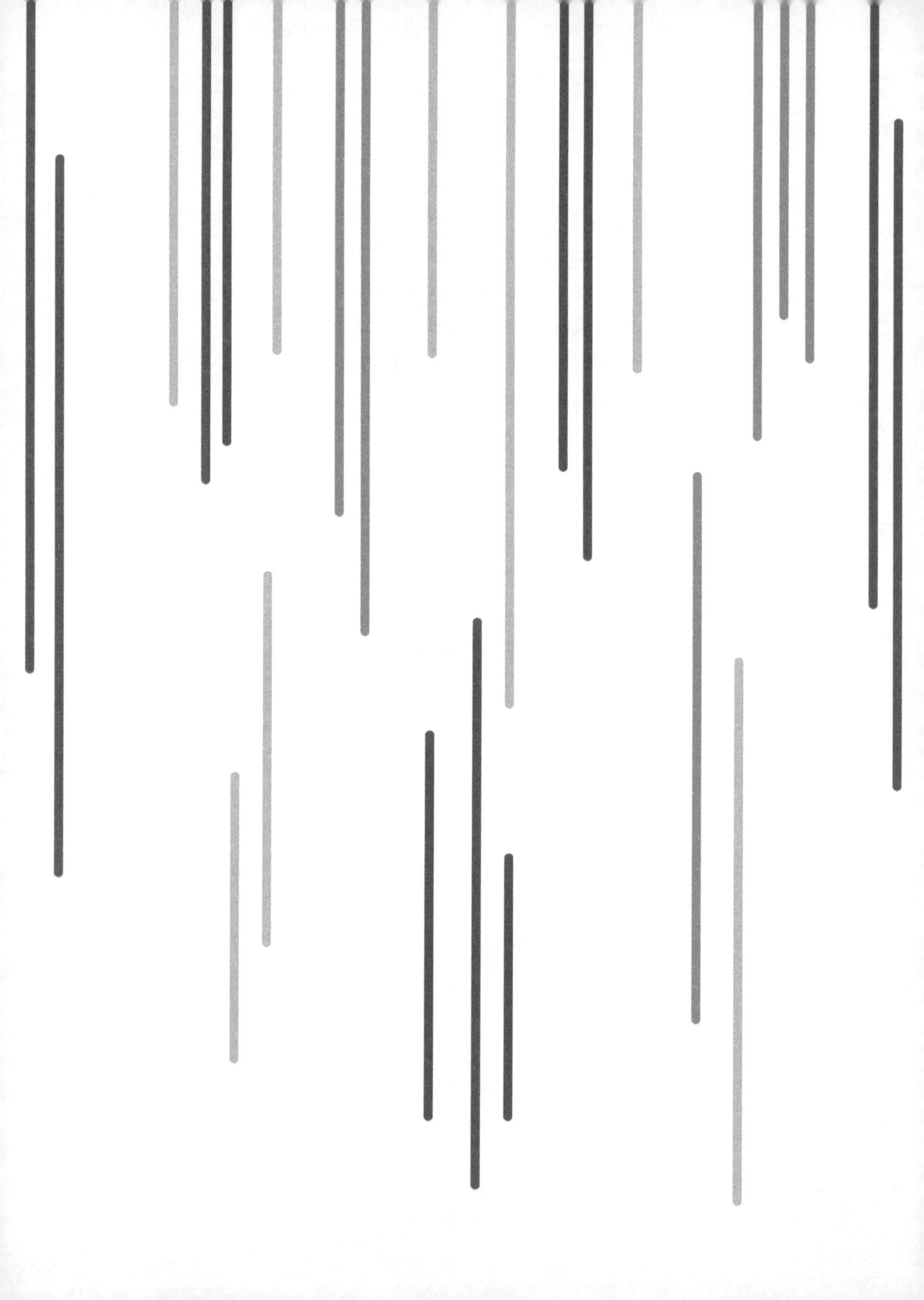

Tonight you are arguing with yourself over whether or not you can fly. You don't have wings, but there's something in you that knows you would just float away over the tops of the buildings, something in you that says, *do it*. It's not a voice, it's a knowing. It's part of you, the part that wants you to jump. There's nothing to distract you up here, on top of the tallest building in a city you may have created with your mind. That's how powerful you are. You built an entire skyline. Surely flying is easy. The knowing knows more than you, it says. But it doesn't say. It's not a voice. It's more assured than that. It's more assured than you, who doubt. No more doubts, it knows. Only the air under your body. You lean forward. You know that soon it won't matter if the knowing is wrong, and the knowledge feels like a great wind inside you.

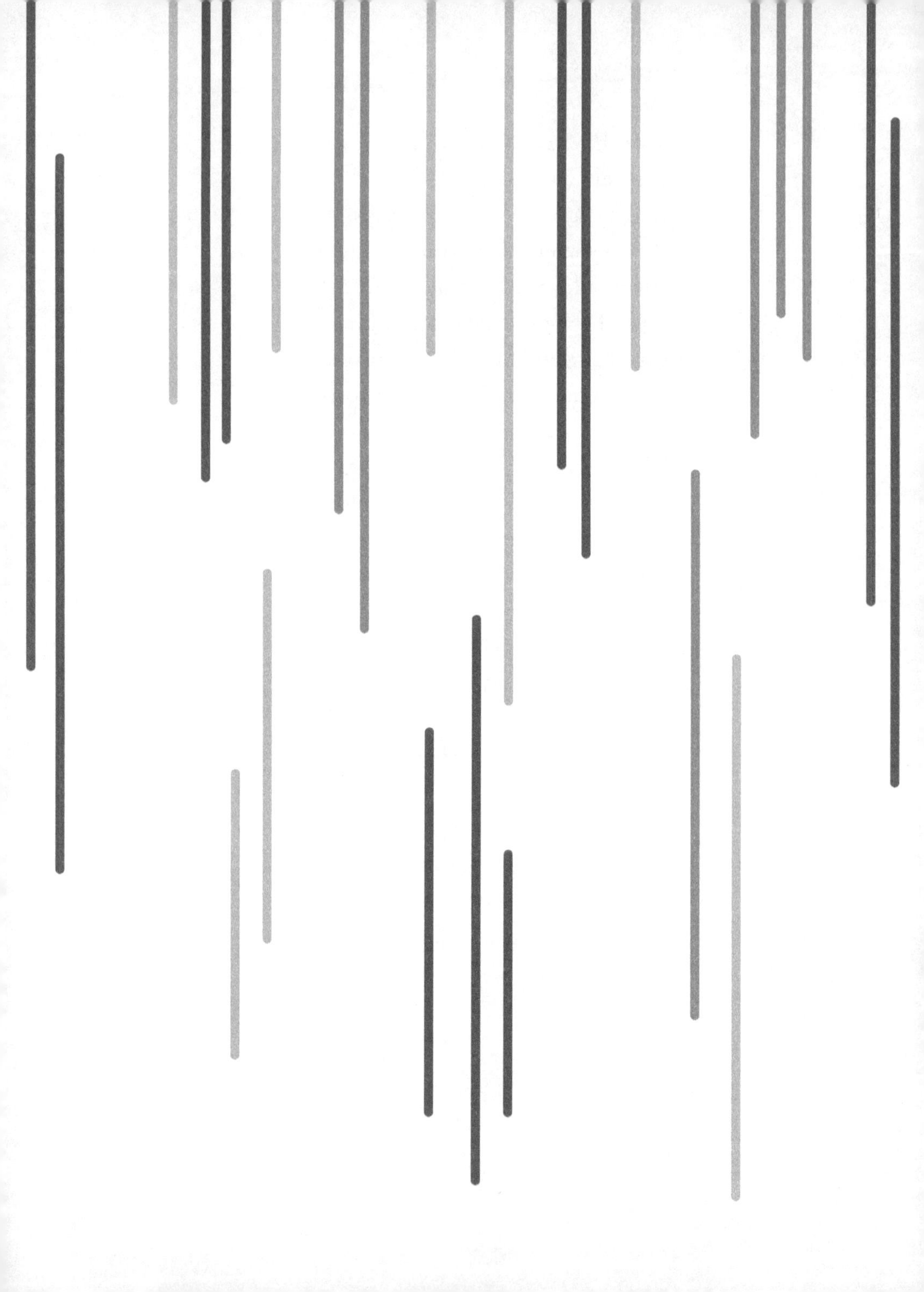

Tonight you are building something, but you don't know what it is. You are in a workshop owned by all the men in your family. That doesn't make sense. That doesn't make it not true. You grip a board and spiders come scrambling over the edge and meld into your hands. Hundreds of spiders pulse under your skin. You shake and shake, but they're in you. What were you building that this happened. What terrible things will you create with hands like these.

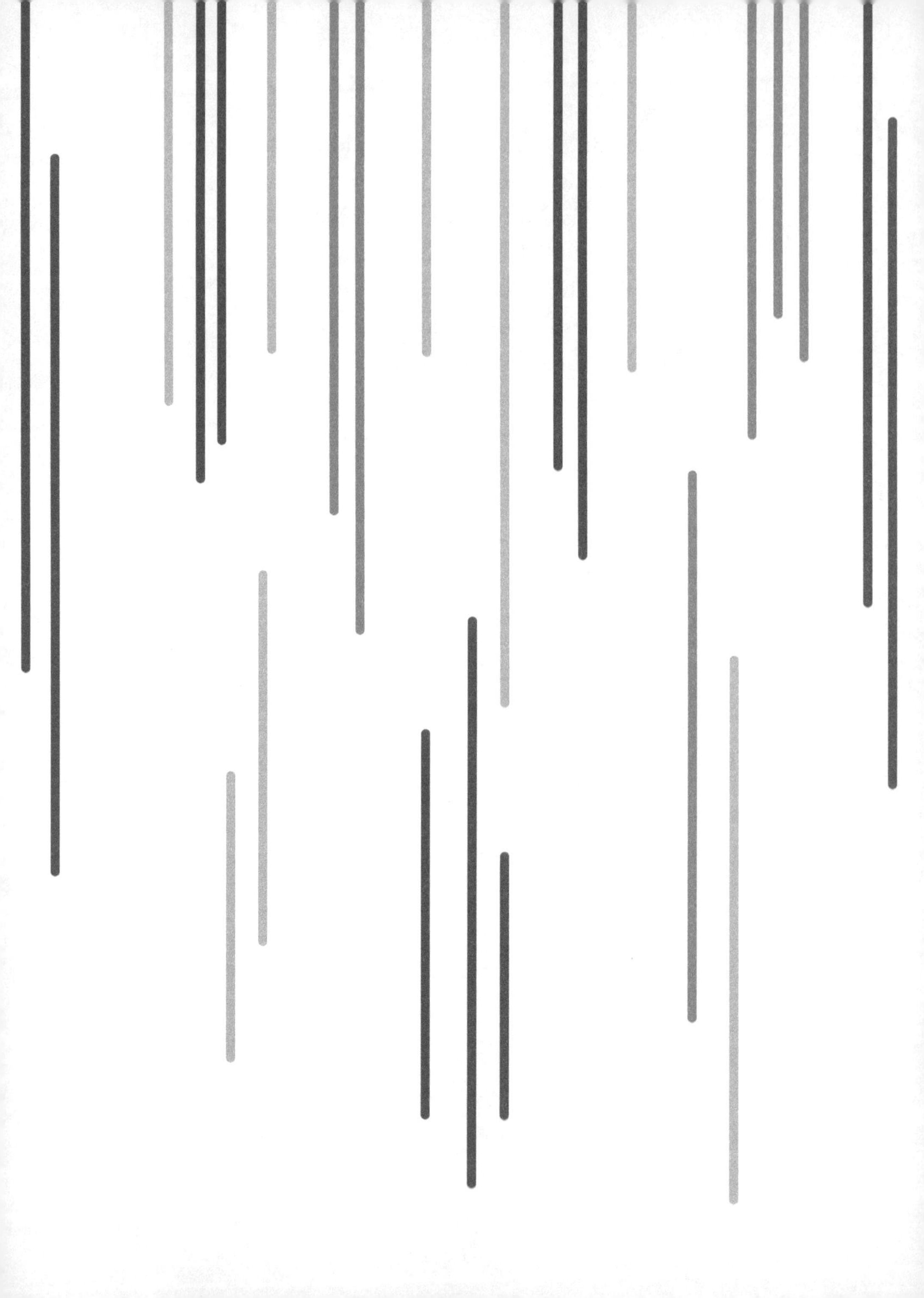

Tonight you are watching the whales migrate southward through the sky, trailing summer behind them. Somewhere north of you, the leaves are already turning red and gold like tropical fish. "Mary Jane's Last Dance" plays out across the landscape, surrounding you, covering you. You put down your drink, take up a diver's position, launch yourself upward, and paddle with your flippers. A dolphin twirls around you, seems to smile. You vaguely recall the coming winter and how something will be taken from you, but the ocean-sky takes the worry and disperses it among schools of tiny sparkles. For now, you float, and you are whole.

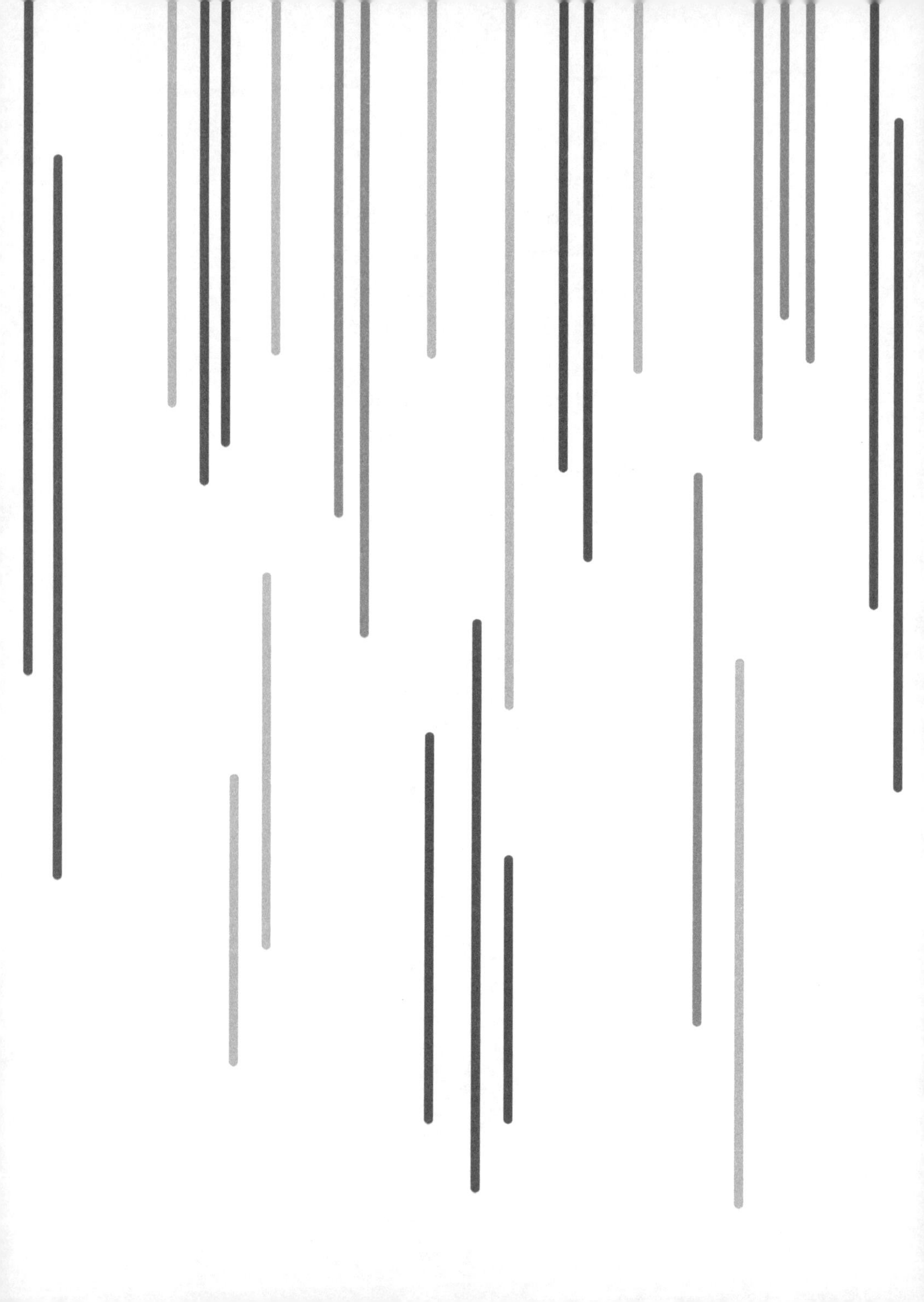

Tonight you are bound in the backwoods. You remember having the wrong bumper sticker, but you don't know what it was. You are hog-tied, cloth-tied in the back of a truck. You can't see, but you hear them talking about the price of corn. You are being driven somewhere, and you can't tell how long the drive takes. The truck sputters to a stop. Doors open and slam. The tailgate creaks, they jump up, you're hefted and tossed. You break every bone in your body when you hit the ground. You hear them digging a hole, and one of them keeps intoning, *Knee high, Fourth of July.* They toss you in, and all your healed bones re-break. Dirt hits your back. You are buried, and you will sprout nevermore. You are planted, and you will rot like your grandfather's barn.

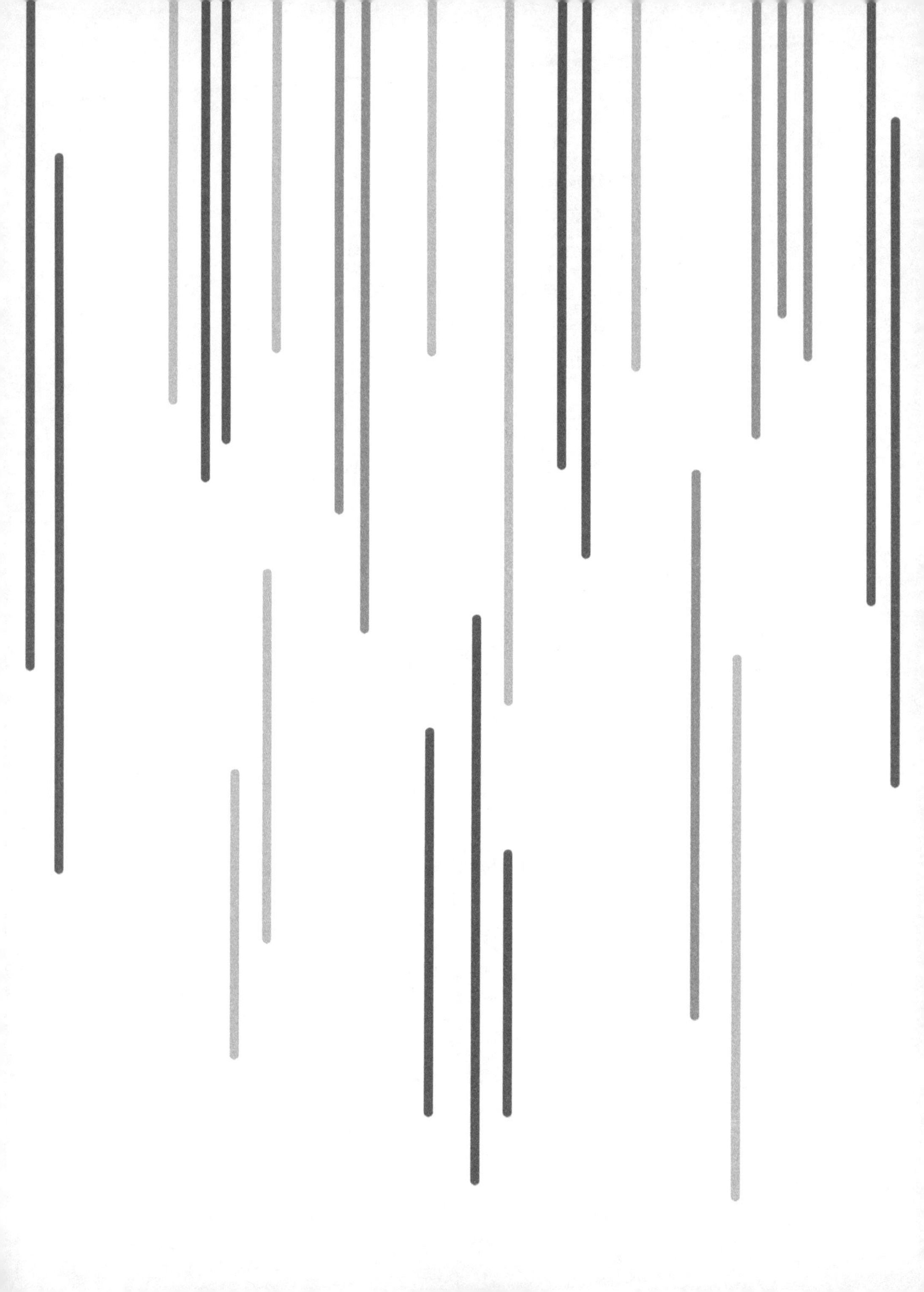

Tonight you are trying your hardest to grow wings. You are earthbound in a field and acutely aware of your shoulder blades. You are grounded in a meadow and pushing muscles out of yourself. You focus on pinpoints, imagine them feathering, fractal your back into updraft. Eyes open, you have no wings but find yourself floating just off the ground. You headstrong yourself an inch upward. You've never concentrated on anything so hard in your life. Another inch. Another inch. You don't know how far you'll get and it doesn't matter. Nobody gave you the means to persist, and even waking can't take it from you.

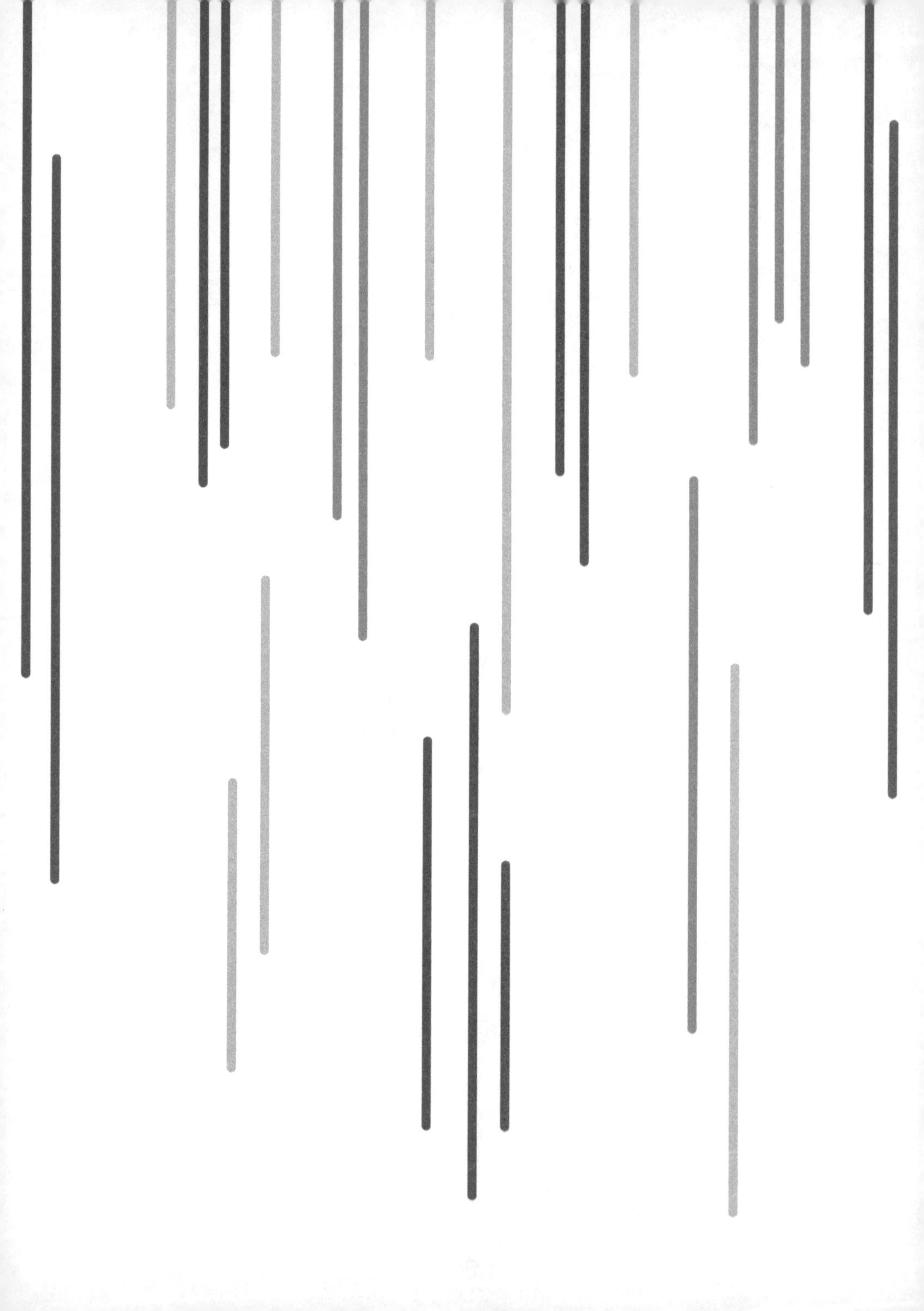

Tonight you are staring in a funhouse mirror at the scar where they took your baby from you. In this one, it's fat. In that one, tall. In the third, you see yourself bashing in your baby's brains and shut your eyes tighter than a stitch. It isn't you, you say. It's your mother, the one who told you she brought you into the world and could take you out of it. You repeat that mantra with trembling lips and crack open one eye. It's a hall of mirrors. It's you and your mother and her mother and so on, ever and ever, not a single break in any surface. You hear them echoing, *It isn't me. It isn't me. It isn't me.*

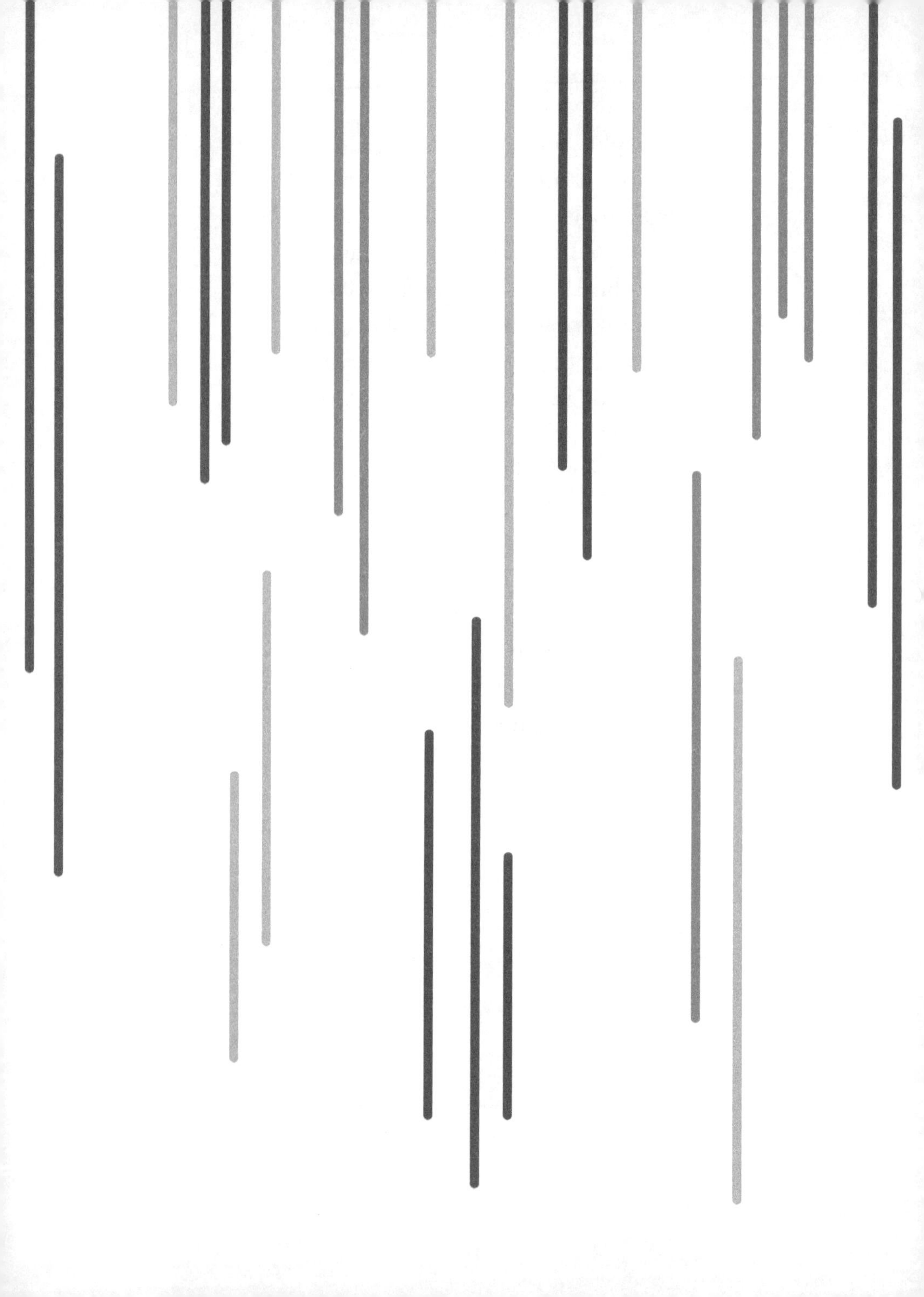

Tonight you are in the last whisky bar at Ragnarök. On a distant field: a wolf, a serpent, a ship made of dead men's nails, the bodies of those you called brothers. Here: a glass. A simple glass. Suntory, anachronistic, not yet invented. The things you find when you're looking for nothing. You sip, and the liquid remains. You drink, and the glass fills. You are draining an ocean swept by storms one gulp at a time. You are exposing the seafloor searching for the bottom. You do not forget where you are and where you are not. You cannot drink enough to forget the thunder is not outside. You'd give both eyes if it meant you'd stop seeing.

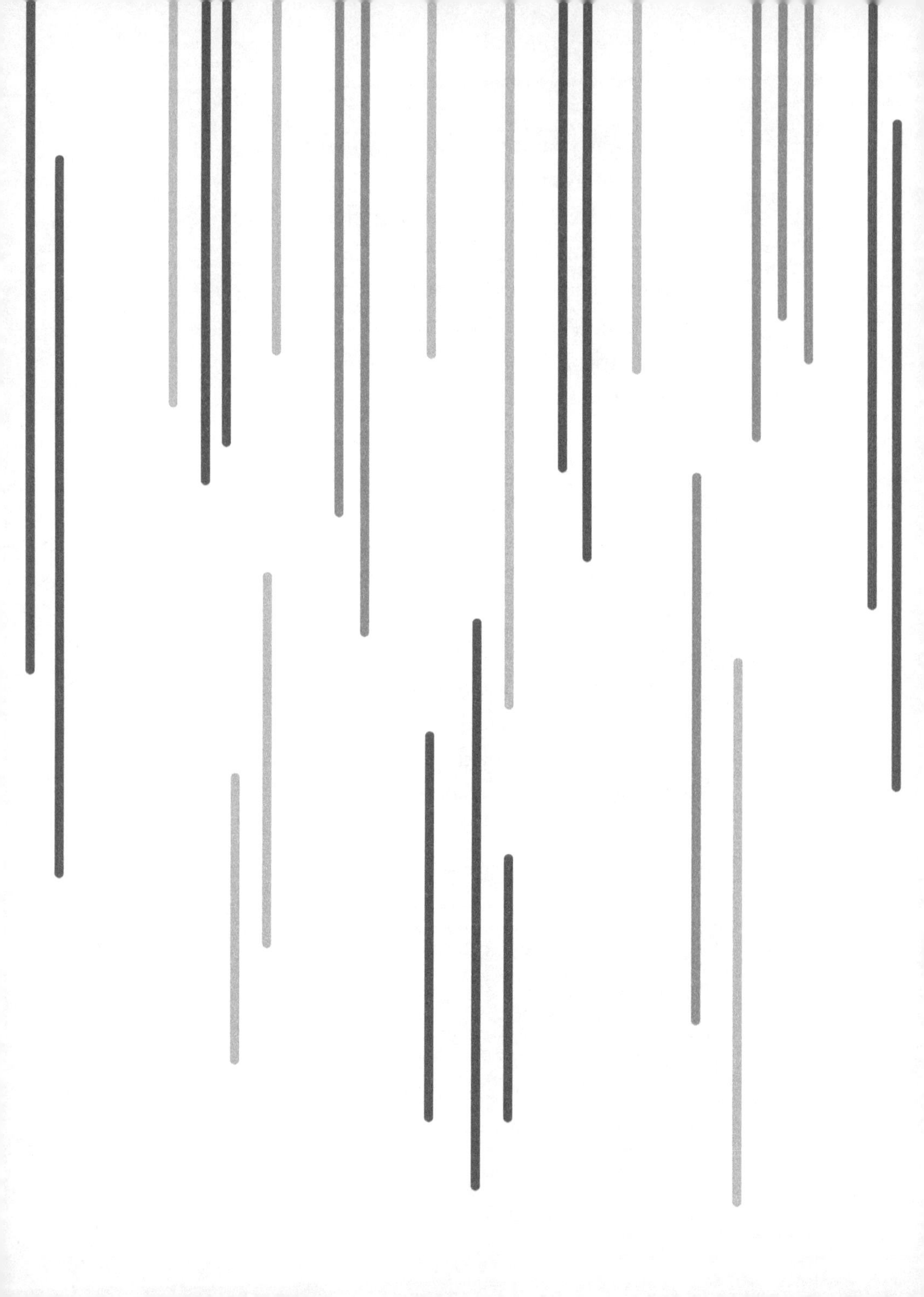

Tonight you are the only human on the plane, the other seats overfilled with things that are tall and covered in fur, jagged tusks and teeth growing from places they don't belong. You are tasty, you're sure, but they don't notice you if you stay very still. You are rabbit-still and rabbit-small. You don't dare look directly at the greenish drool leaking from the mouth of the thing next to you, its arm almost touching yours. You are thirty thousand feet from safety, trying not to exhale. The thing next to you shifts, and you know you'll have to prove you're not human. You bite down on your forearm, suck the blood up and choke it down. The rest of the things begin to tear at themselves, bellow and scream and tear, tear, tear. You cower and recall the spell you taught yourself as a child: *If I hurt myself first, they can't get to me.*

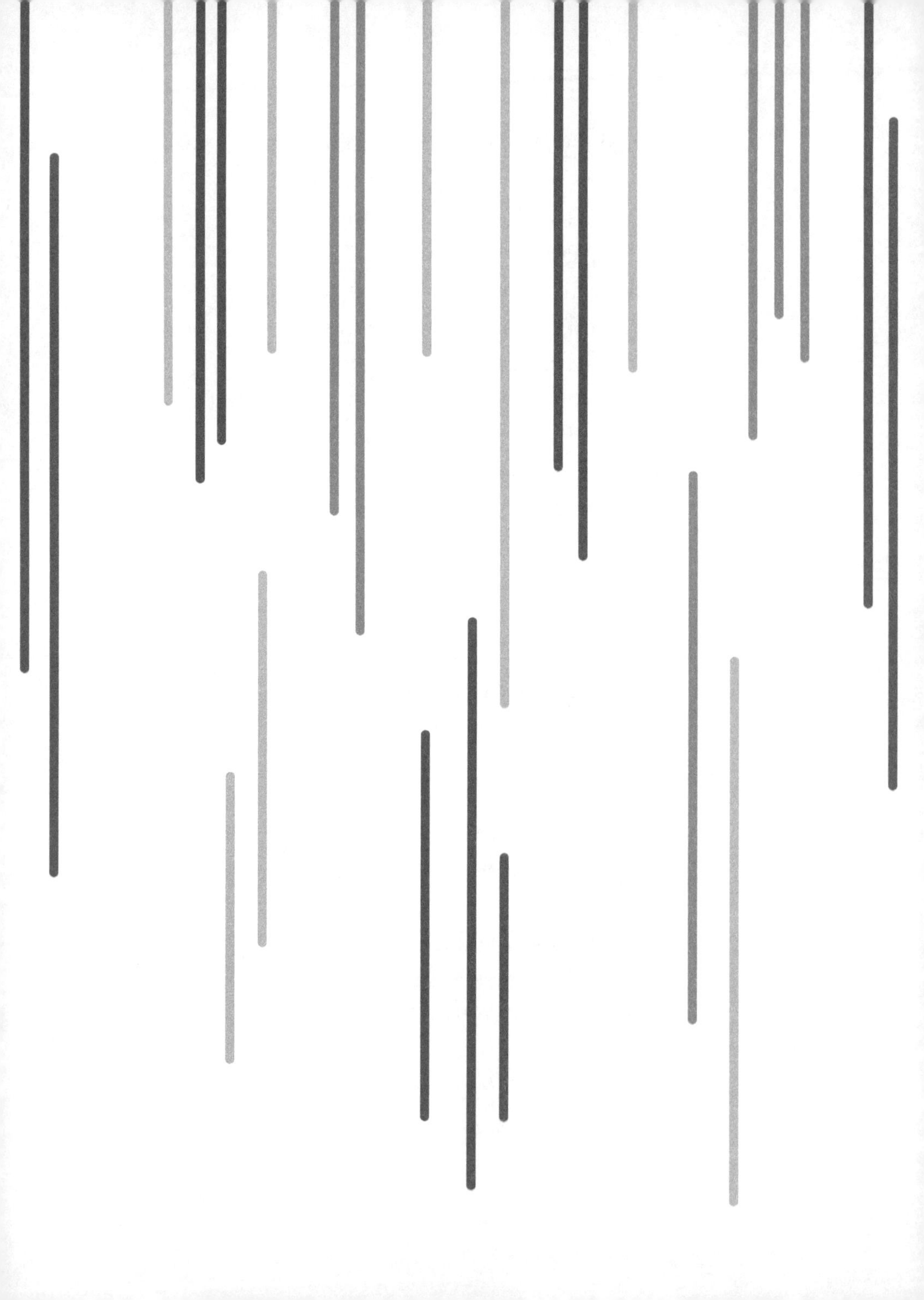

Tonight you are paddling a canoe in the middle of the ocean, precisely midway in the Atlantic. You are vaguely aware ocean and canoe are anagrams for each other. You heard that somewhere, and you feel like it's come back to mock you now. Here. Now. Nowhere. The stars are out tonight, a thing to behold. You feel fake, made out of paper, constructed, a concert of dust. Something is wrong. You're not moving. That's not quite right. You're moving two directions at once and canceling both out. The waves form a random pile that you swear is perfectly ordered. You are Gs, As, Ts, and Cs, an incomplete alphabet spilling into the soup of the sea. Your canoe dissolves. You do, too. You are everywhere at once, a riddle for poets or theoretical physicists. At some level, you think, before all thinking ceases, there's not so much difference between those fields. At some level, you think, the possibilities outweigh the real.

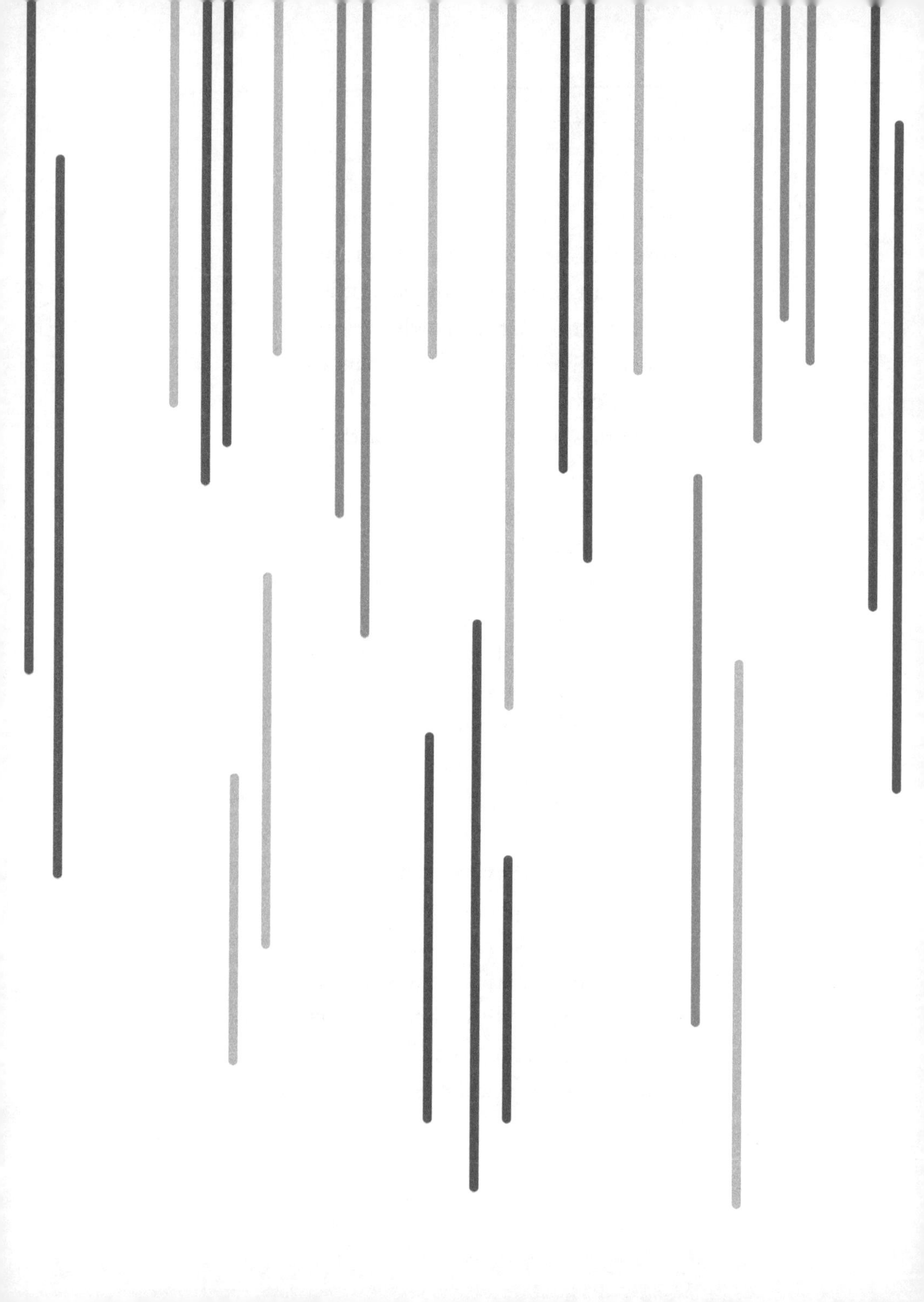

Tonight you are waiting for the elementary school children to cross, when a man steps out of a van and turns the crosswalk into a war zone. You think, *This can't be happening* very clearly and process the bursts of blood not clearly at all and something clicks and you hit the gas, plow into him with your car. You're in shock. You think to yourself *I'm in shock.* You're in shock. One of the children rises, and the hairs on the back of your neck go up. *That kid is dead*, you think, seeing through the chest wound. Another child pulls himself to his feet, the top of his head a scene from a movie or a place very far away but *Please not here.* They are standing and shambling and surrounding you. *I've made a mistake*, you think, and you know you'll die. You know everything that is about to happen. Before they claim you, you just want to know if they have been like this all along or if you are being punished because you should have done something sooner. The answer is standing just outside your door, shaped like a hole in a child.

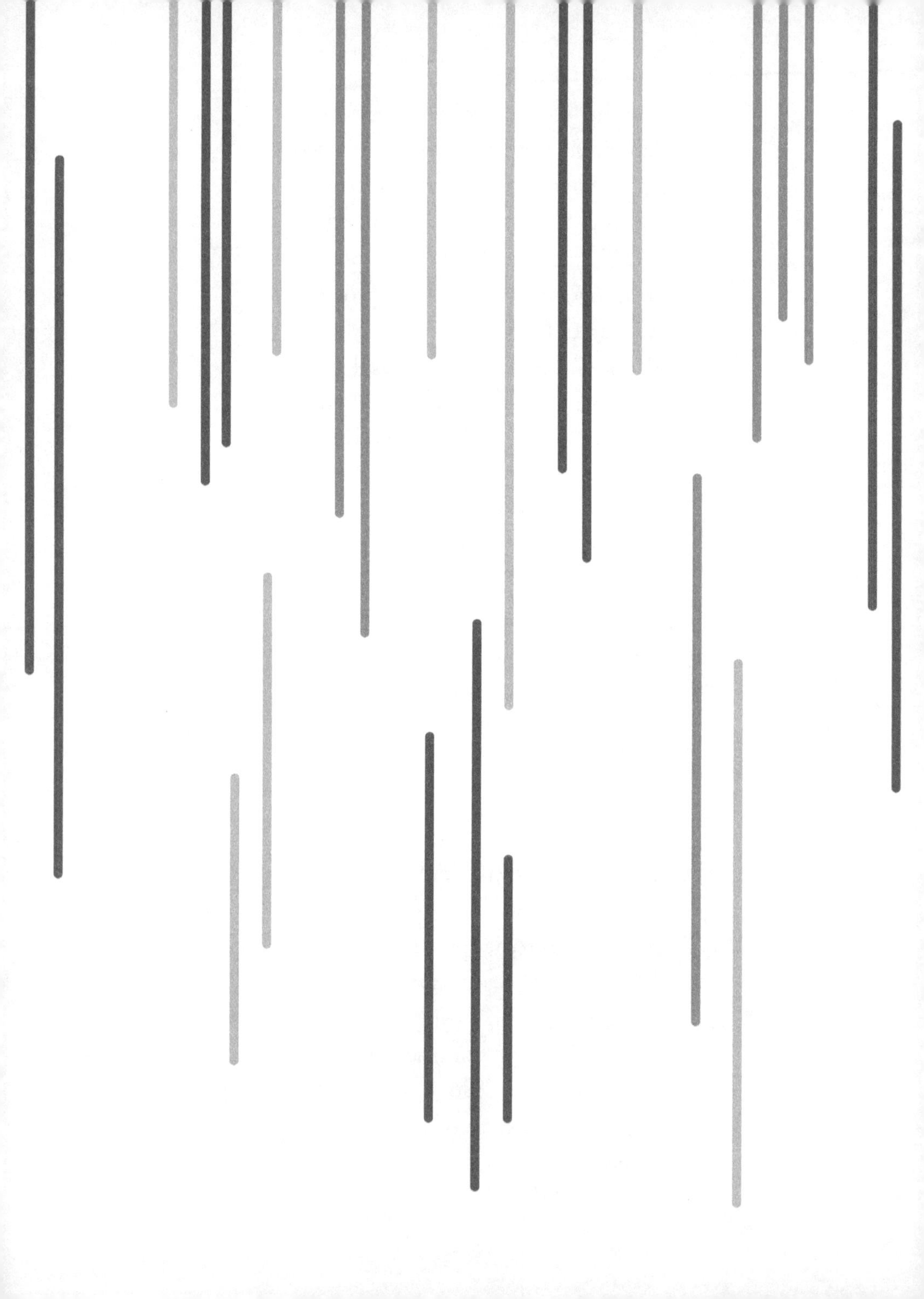

Tonight you are seated in a darkened tent, across from a skeleton selecting Tarot cards. The skeleton has a perpetual smile. It lays them in front of you, and every one is Death. No Lovers. No Tower. Just Deaths in a row. The skeleton leans in, *This is all I can promise you.* You pick up the deck and stack it in a house of cards. There, you've made The Tower. You arrange them in a heart. Lovers. It's true, you realize, all Fate will deal you is death, but you can do with the knowledge what you will.

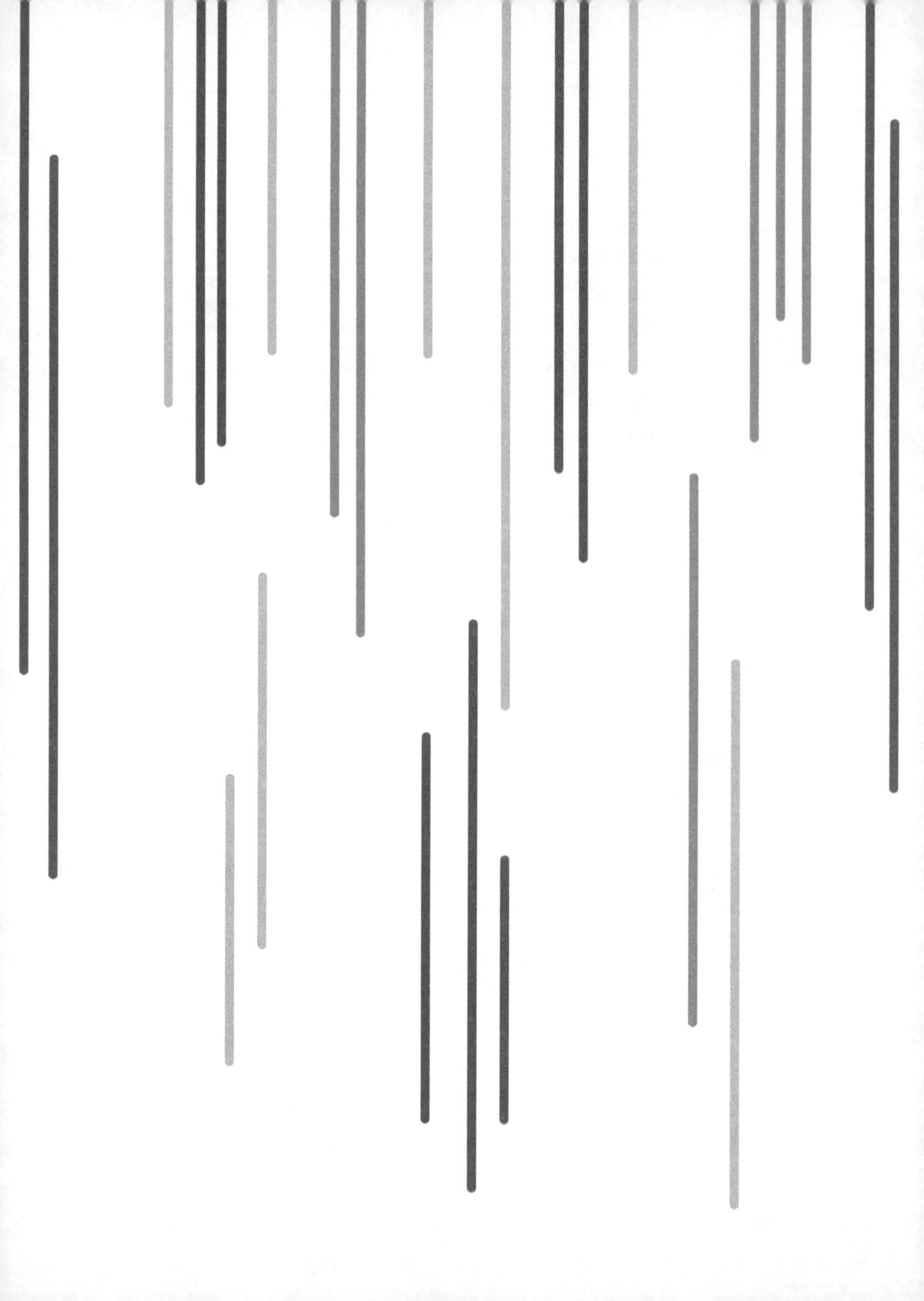

Tonight you are making dangerous art. Your spray paint springs to life like fireflies on brick. Every misrepresented friend you've ever known, every downtrodden icon. You are populating the sides of buildings with the histories they tore from your books. You are working faster than they can sandblast pride. You are swirl of pressurization and hiss, and the buildings themselves begin to come alive, grow heads and arms and legs and more, rise out of cement foundations and walk. You are leading downtown down its own main avenue, a parade of those who refuse to be erased.

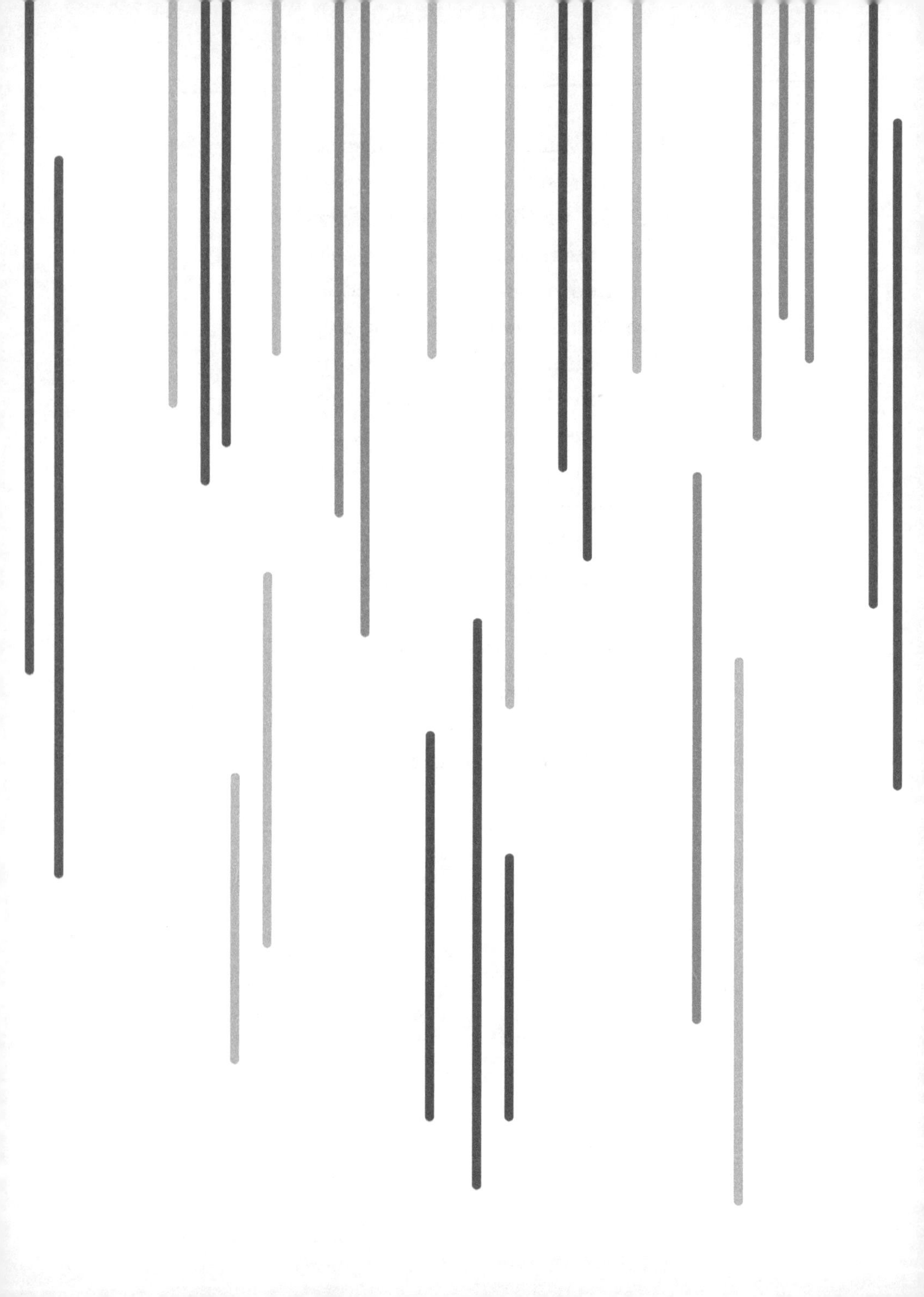

Tonight you are plowing through clouds of locusts on a motorcycle. There is a frog on your windshield catching bugs with its tongue. You cross a river of blood on a bridge that's a snake. The sun is a wheel with eyes. Your beard is long as God's and flailing behind you, your sunglasses are on, your arms outstretched to the handlebars. You are riding behind the four bikers of the apocalypse, trailing mercy in your wake. You are the Angel of the Second Chance, and your radio is tuned to the music of the spheres.

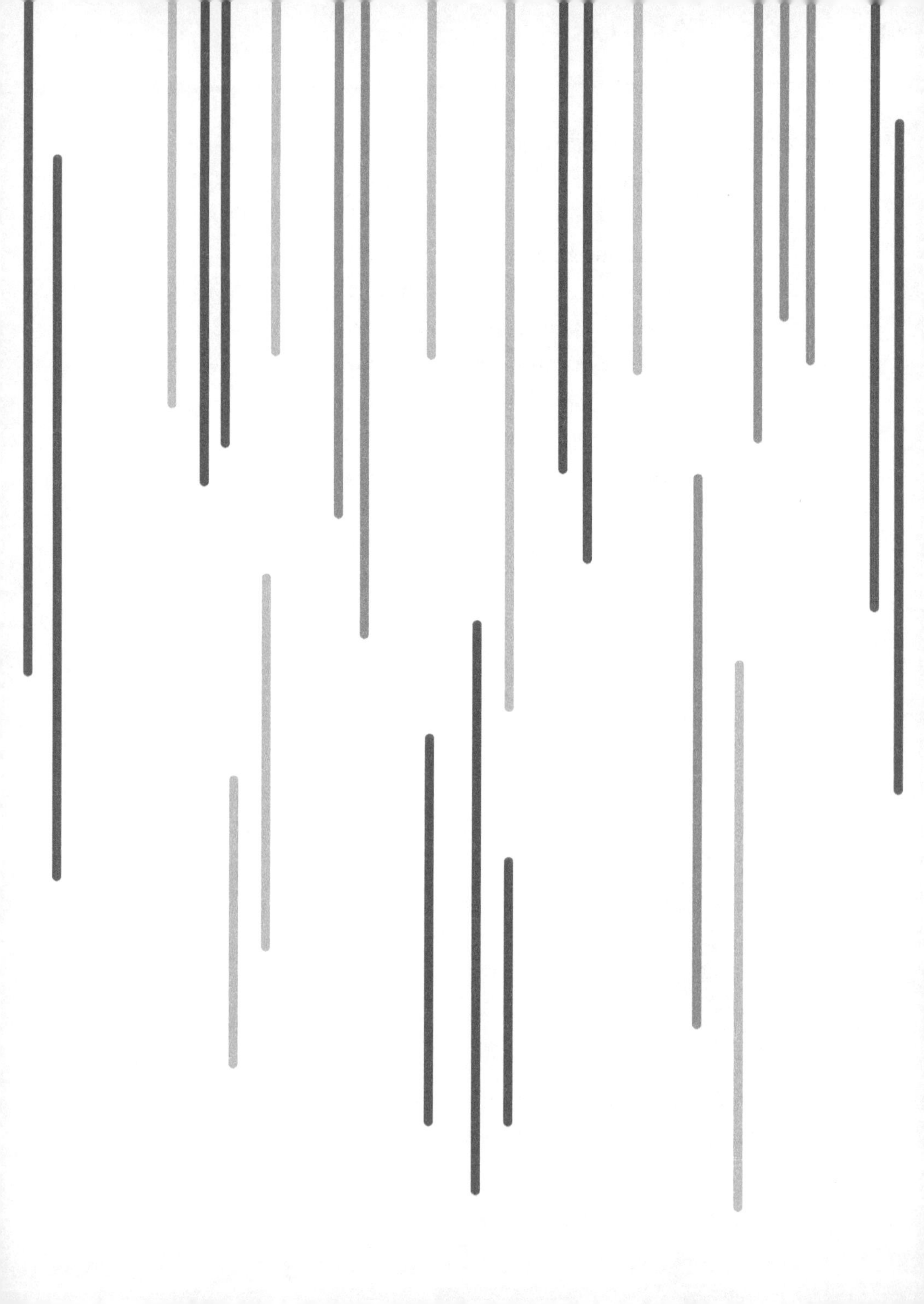

Tonight you are faster than an
avalanche,   downward-bound
on a snowboard, powder acting
anime around you, a great wave
off the Himalayas in pursuit,
you untouchable on the slope,
roadrunner to snow's coyote, so
lightning your body leaves your
consciousness behind to watch it
speed away, down a mountain, up
the next, trailing clouds, exuberant.

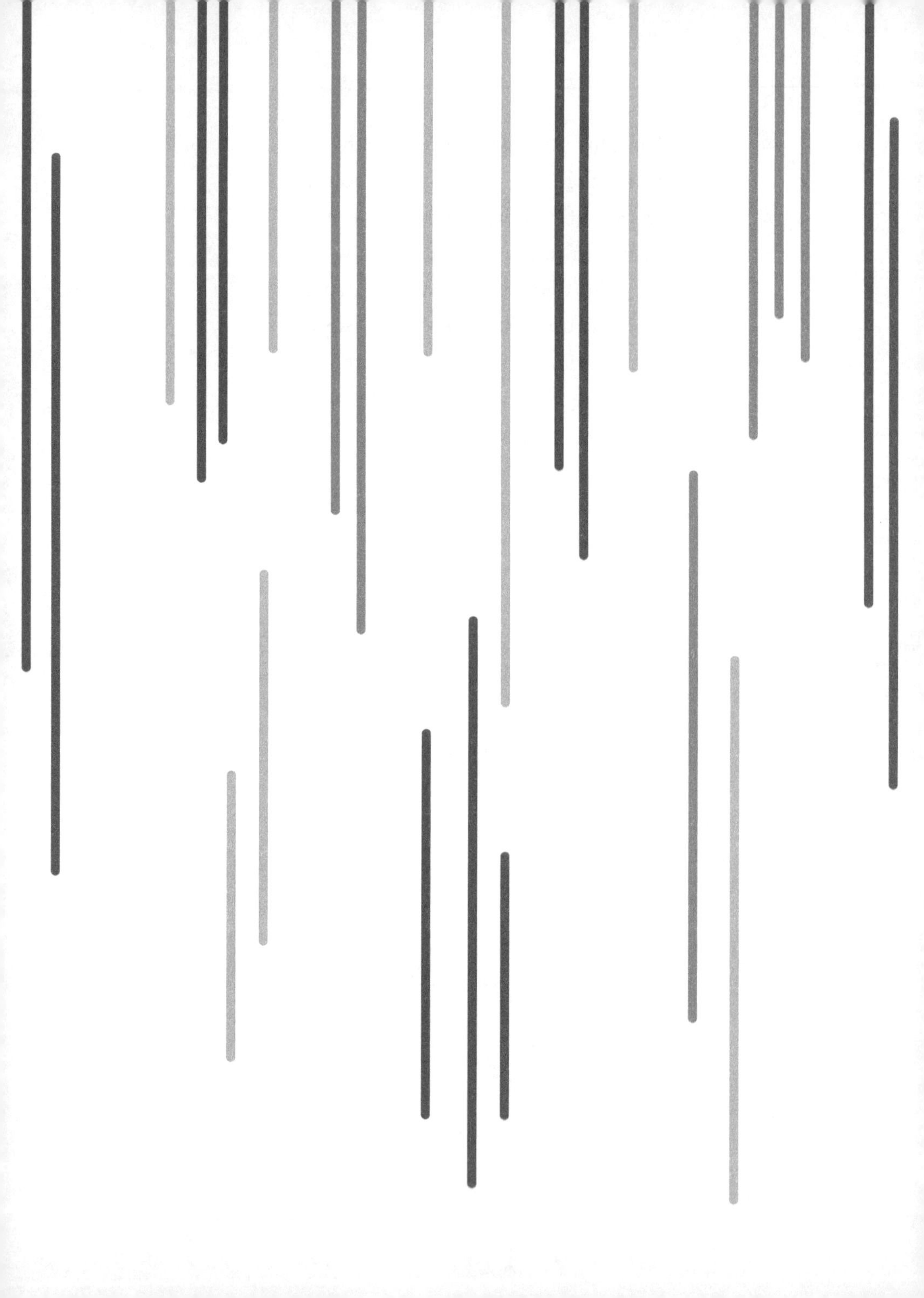

Tonight you are crucified on a long stretch of ancient road, the wooden Ts stretching out in either direction as far as you can see. You don't remember if you all rebelled. As far as you can tell, you've always been up here, cradle to grave. The man to your right asks you if you remember the names of the gods, and you tell him *timber* and *eagle*. The man to your left is food for ravens. There is a TV on the ground in front of you. You are surprised you know what a TV is. A man is on the news reporting on the economy, blaming the shortage of nails on your hands.

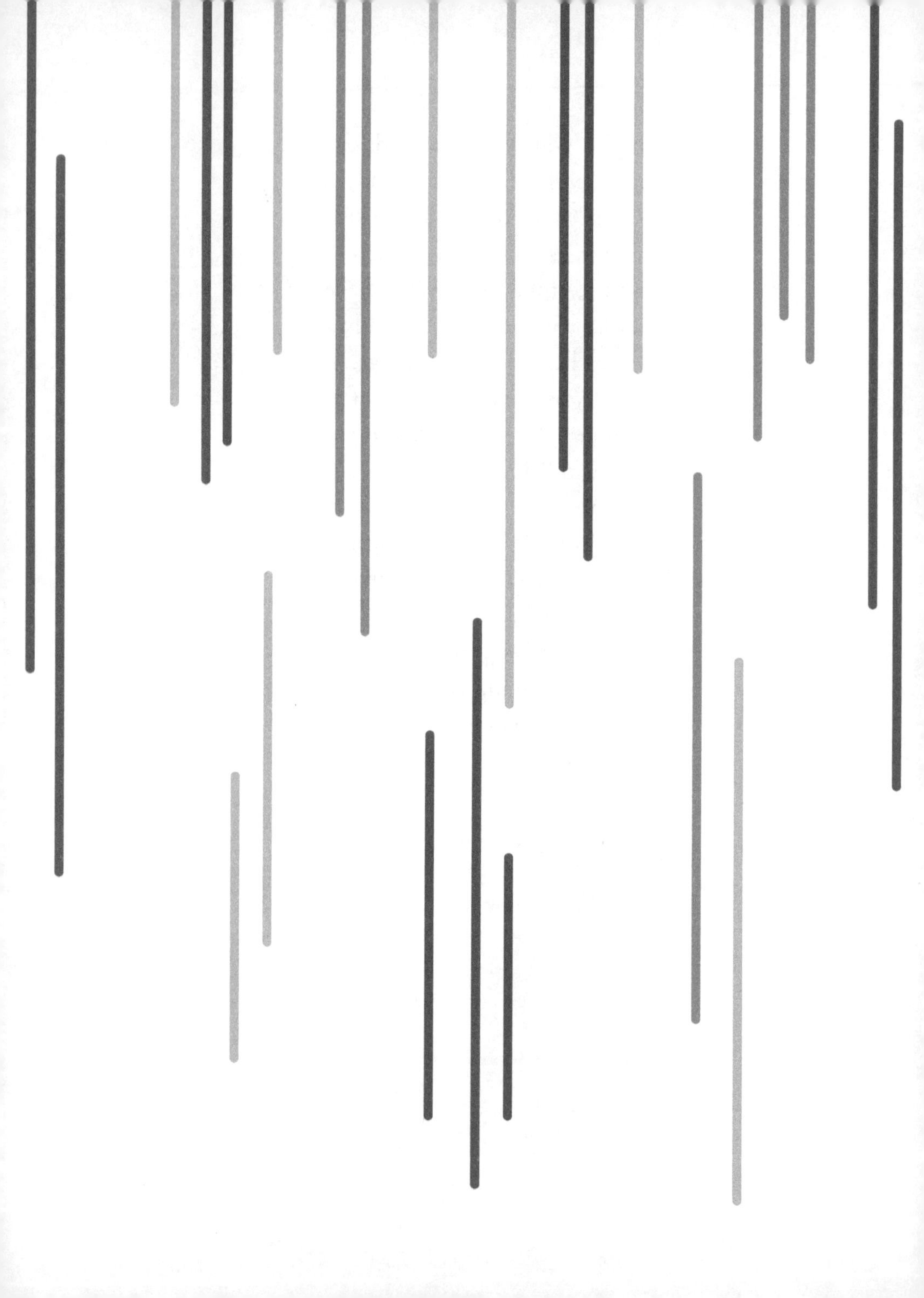

Tonight you are a heart attack on stilettos. You *vavoom* past a theater on 12th and appear on every screen inside. Every hot dog in the corner cart cooks without water. Passersby spin so fast the energy turns on all the lights in the city. You are illumination in drag, the great goddess Apolla. A drunk catcalls you, and the words come out like an Apollinaire poem. You catch them between long pink nails, roll them into a cigarette, walk off smoking *Hey, sexy lady,* like it was a compliment you were looking for all along.

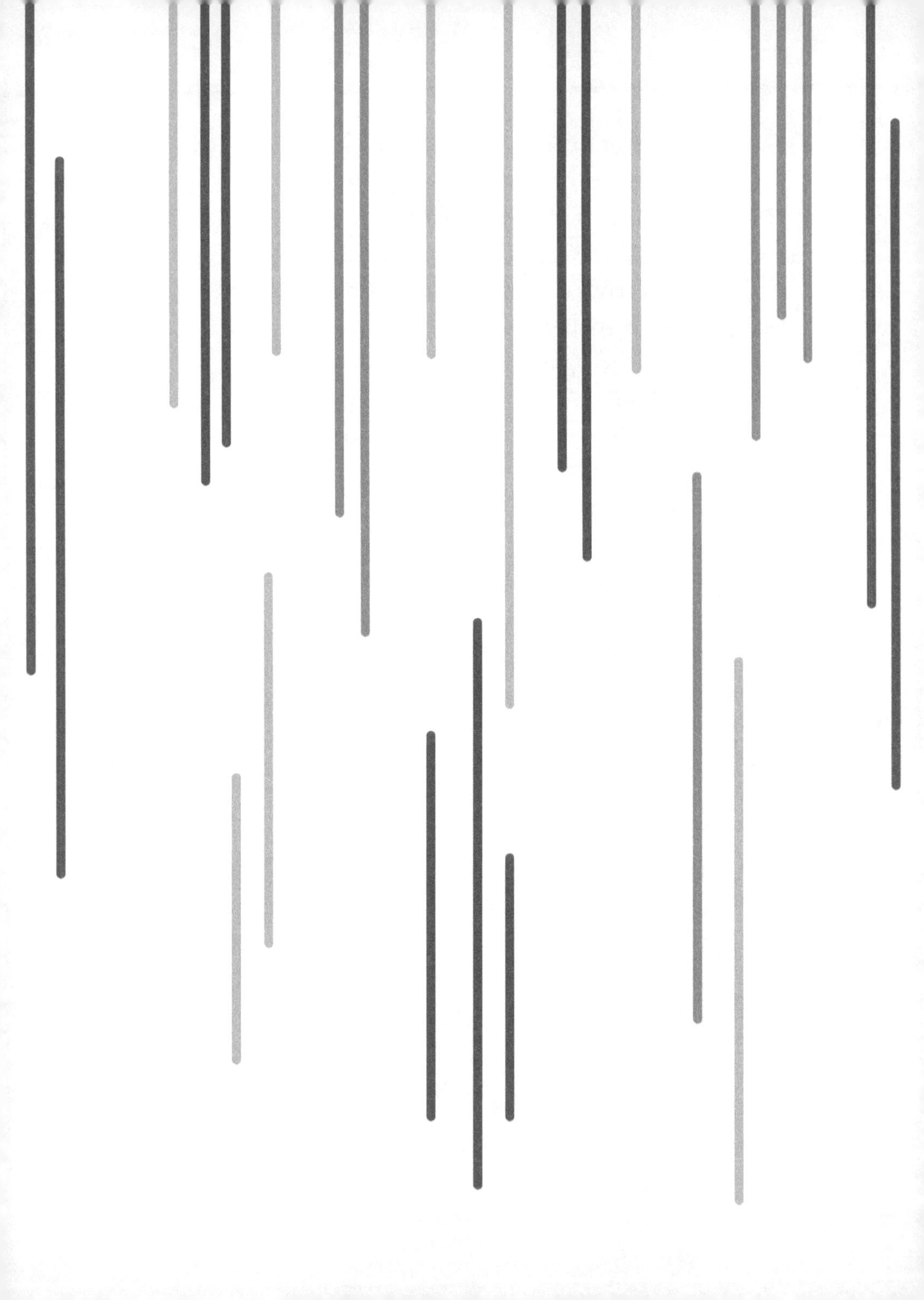

Tonight you are tusked, pearl-watcher, spear in your side and headlong. You are forest-crasher, trample and snort, awkward as elephant with goldfish memory. You are gorilla pounding, whale at the surface come crashing onto boats. You are eagle-eyed, scent-heavy as a dog, forked tongue prepared to offer apples. Every liter of blood in your veins tells you this is no evil, just awakening to a howled moon. The wise men call you fool, but they have never seen a man as beautiful as the one who stands before you.

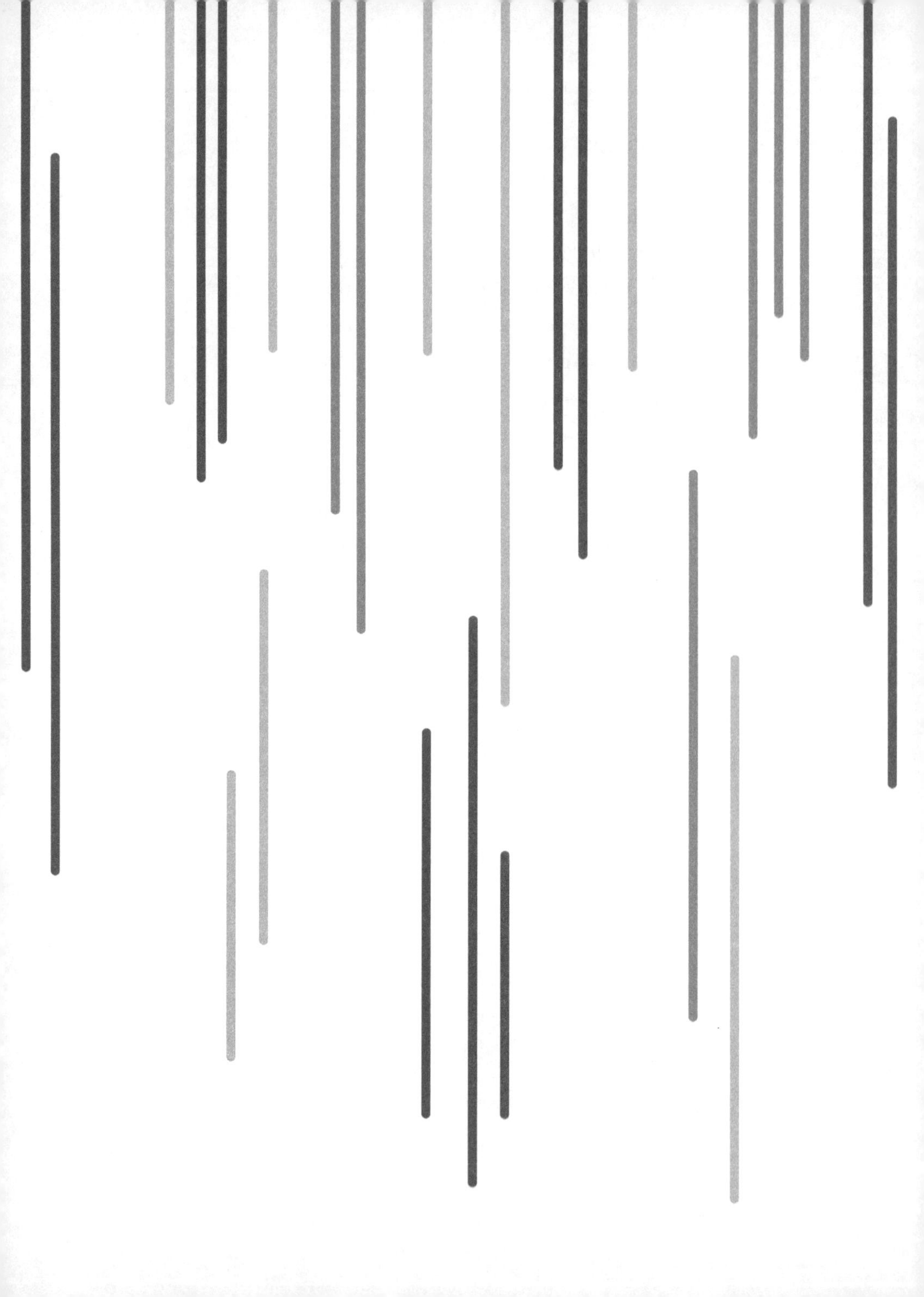

Tonight you are between rows of blueberry bushes, pulling the fruit into a bucket hung around your neck. You reach out with both hands, massage each grouping, let them roll between your arms and plink. You pop one into your mouth. You pick one, eat one. Pick one, eat two. You reach out with both hands, massage a bundle of blueberries and trickle them into your palms. You devour the whole handful. You belch, and somewhere a donkey kicks. You giggle, and the breeze smells like churned butter for an instant. You shrink and unslip the bucket's harness, leap into a bush, your insect wings fluttering. You await the next picker with an armful of berries into which you have scratched the words *mischief* and *joy*.

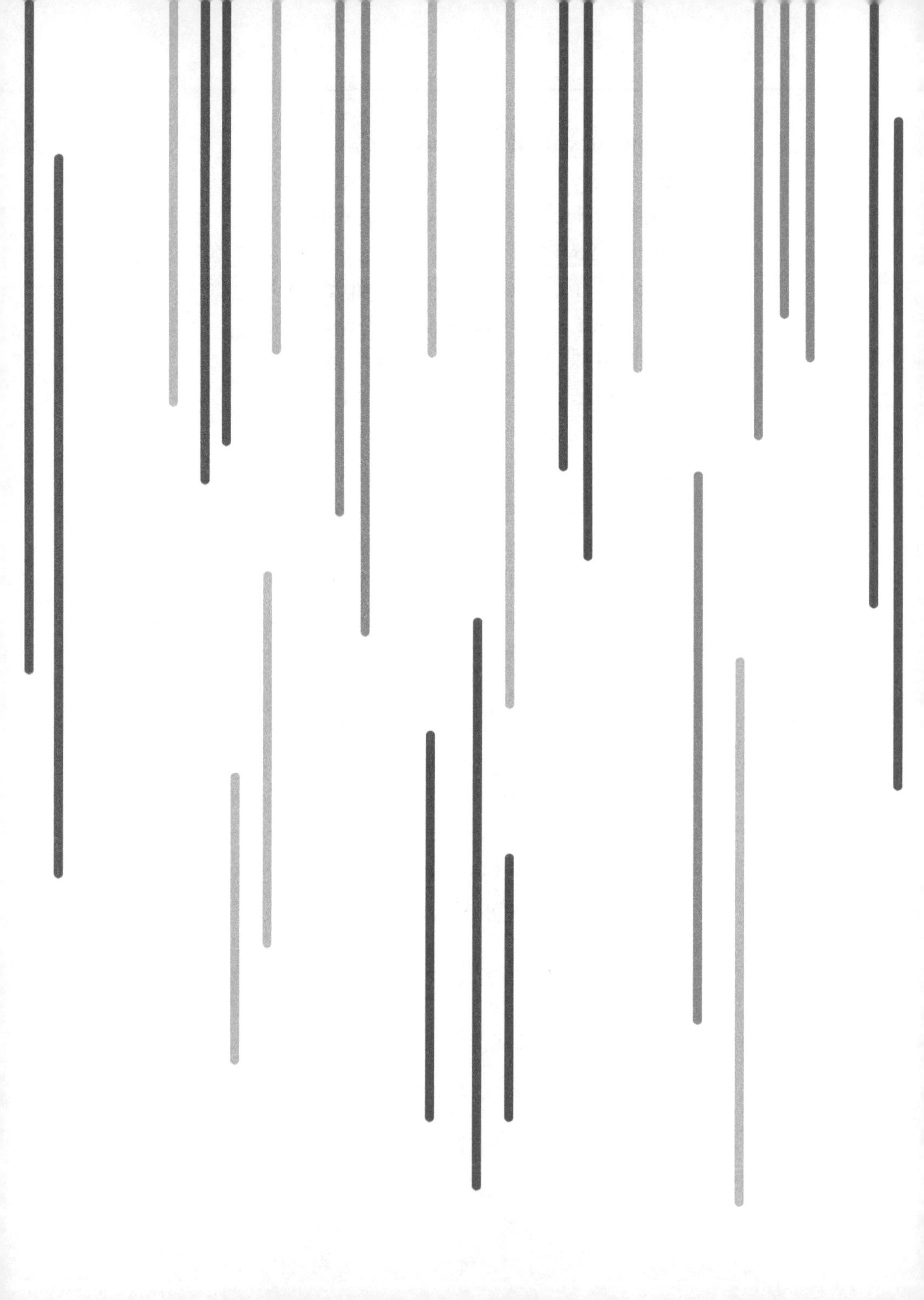

Tonight you are the tenth child of a tenth child, tracing your family tree painted on a wall like a mural. It has real branches growing out of the brick, birds nesting in your cousins' names. There's a window where your grandparents belong, and through it you can see the ocean. You're in a warehouse on a dock where people come to begin a new life. Across the waters, there is a building like this with a mural that continues this one. You could look through every window and never run out of visions. You could cross every ocean and still not find your roots.

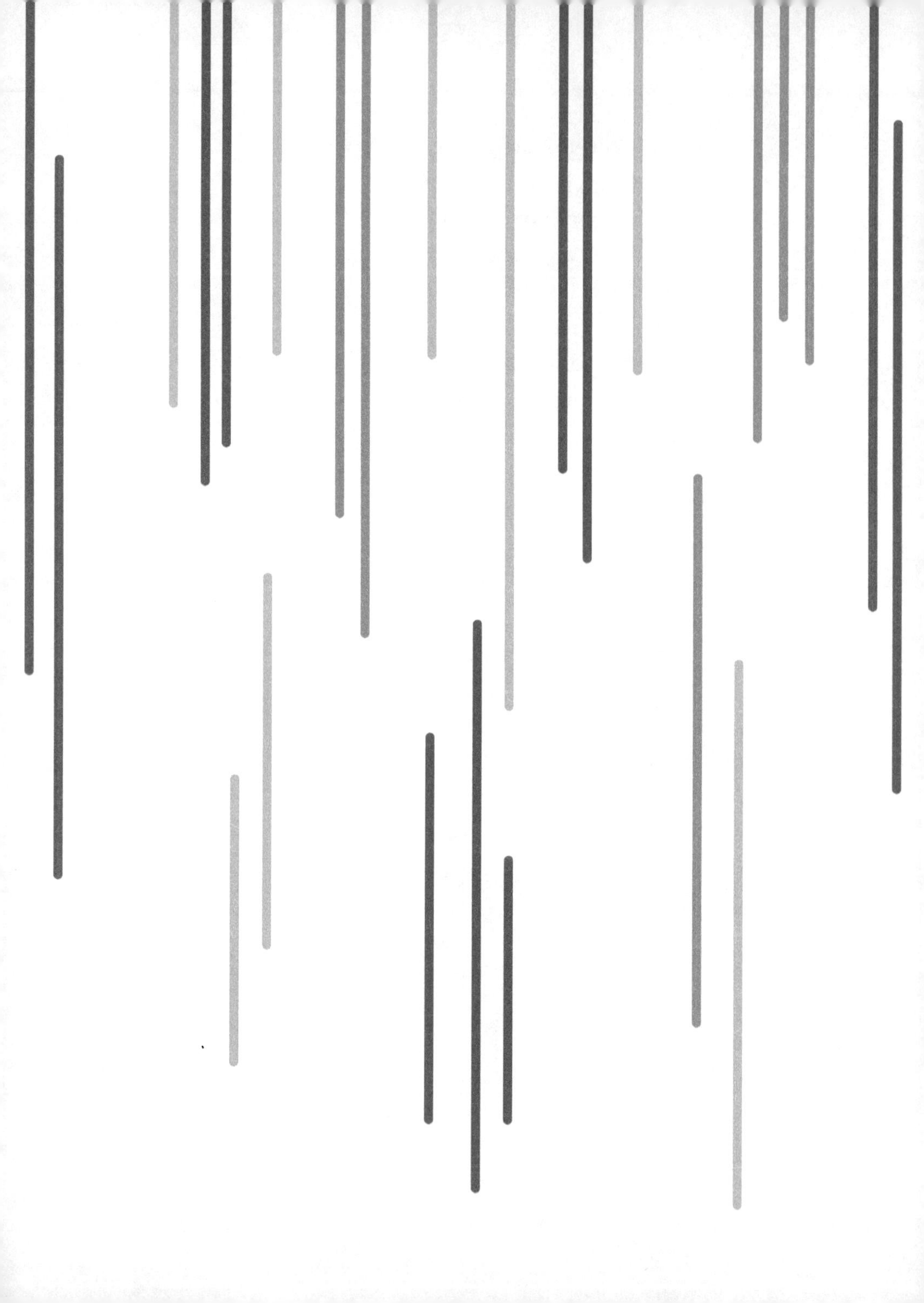

Tonight you are in the market of violence under the sign of dirt. *Bury your dead*, you offer, *bury your dead*. The assassins slink past you. The king's men are too proud. You try to make eye contact, are flipped the finger by gangbangers. Not the soldiers nor the jihadists, not the made men nor the pigs. Nobody is buying what you have to offer. No one hides the bodies here. What use is a coverup when everyone is culpable? Who cares for a grave when the money is in killing?

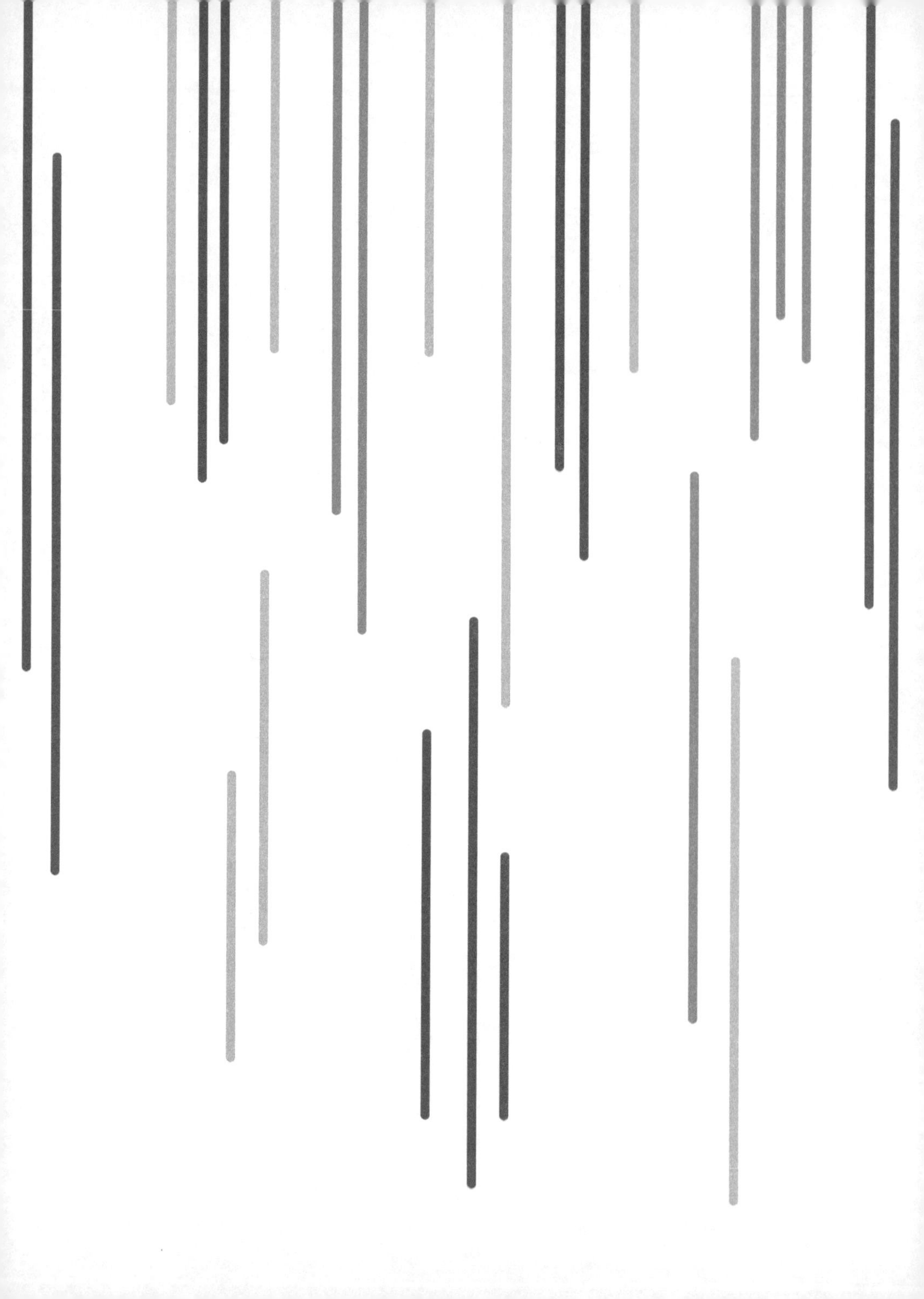

Tonight you are seated at the base of a tree in the desert. You hold a clay bowl full of water. The tree seasons in an instant—*flower leaves falling bare*. It repeats. It repeats. One of the flowers spirals down and lands in your bowl. You think, *I have invented tea.* A pause. *The tree has invented tea.* The world is heating up, spring shortening every cycle. The tree is dying, but you have already drunk your tea. The tree needs. You focus and exhale, turn to water and absorb into the soil. You are a tree in the desert, a clay bowl at your roots. Your trunk carries a hint of human memory, that some god of sacrifice was also harbinger of rebirth.

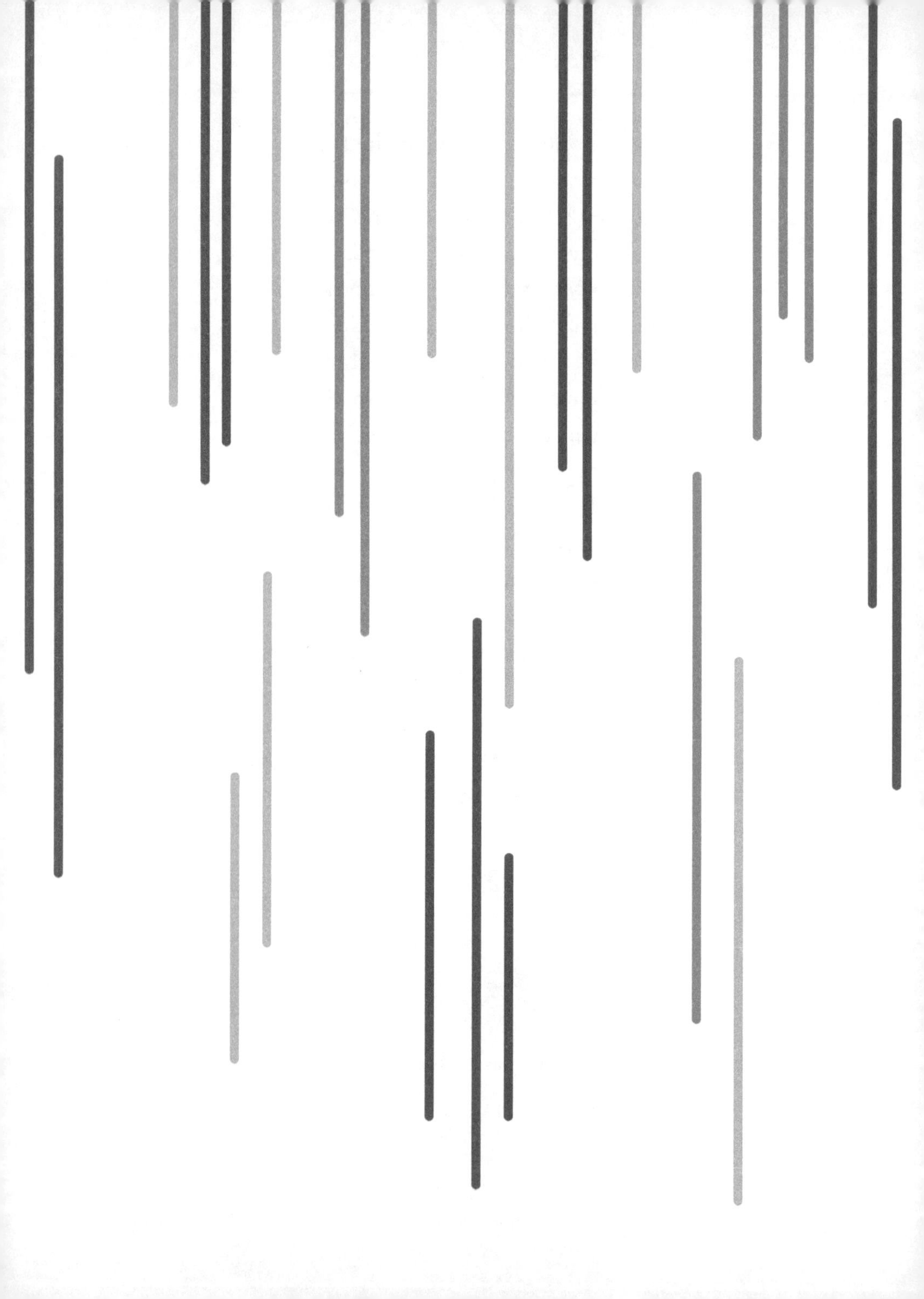

Tonight you don't know why they're taking your dog away. You loved him. You love him. He's only bitten you a few times. You don't know how many times he's bitten you, but he didn't mean to. You're sure of it. You're sure no other dog would be as good to you. You can't even picture another dog. You can't picture him now. You're alone in a room with no doors and no windows and no mirrors and no dog and no idea what to do. It's just you in the room, staring at your arms as they ooze and seal, open and close. You don't remember how to hold anything with them. Without the bite marks, you don't even think you'd recognize your own hands.

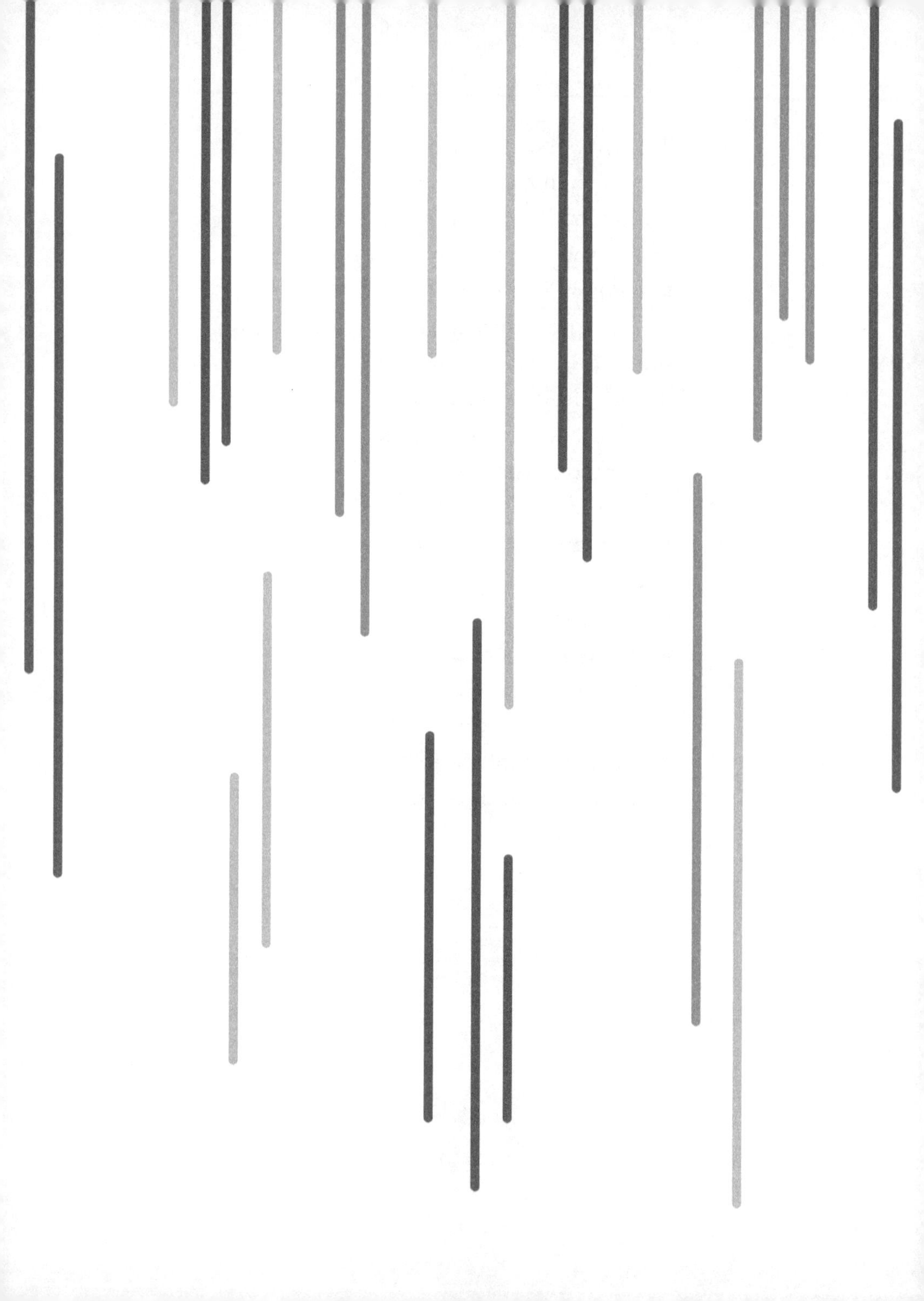

Tonight you are walking in the deep woods singing *la la la la,* when a branch falls on your head. You bite off your tongue, and it falls to the ground and begins inching away like a worm. Your blood aerosolizes, becomes a swarm of bees bursting from your mouth. The branch is an alligator hissing. The trees crouch down to look at you, *intruder.* You think back to a textbook you once read, try to shout, *I'm a biome, too,* but it comes out as a cloud of flies. Everything is going dark. You cover yourself with mud. You are planting yourself like a wildflower soon to sleep, soon to dream of a bursting spring.

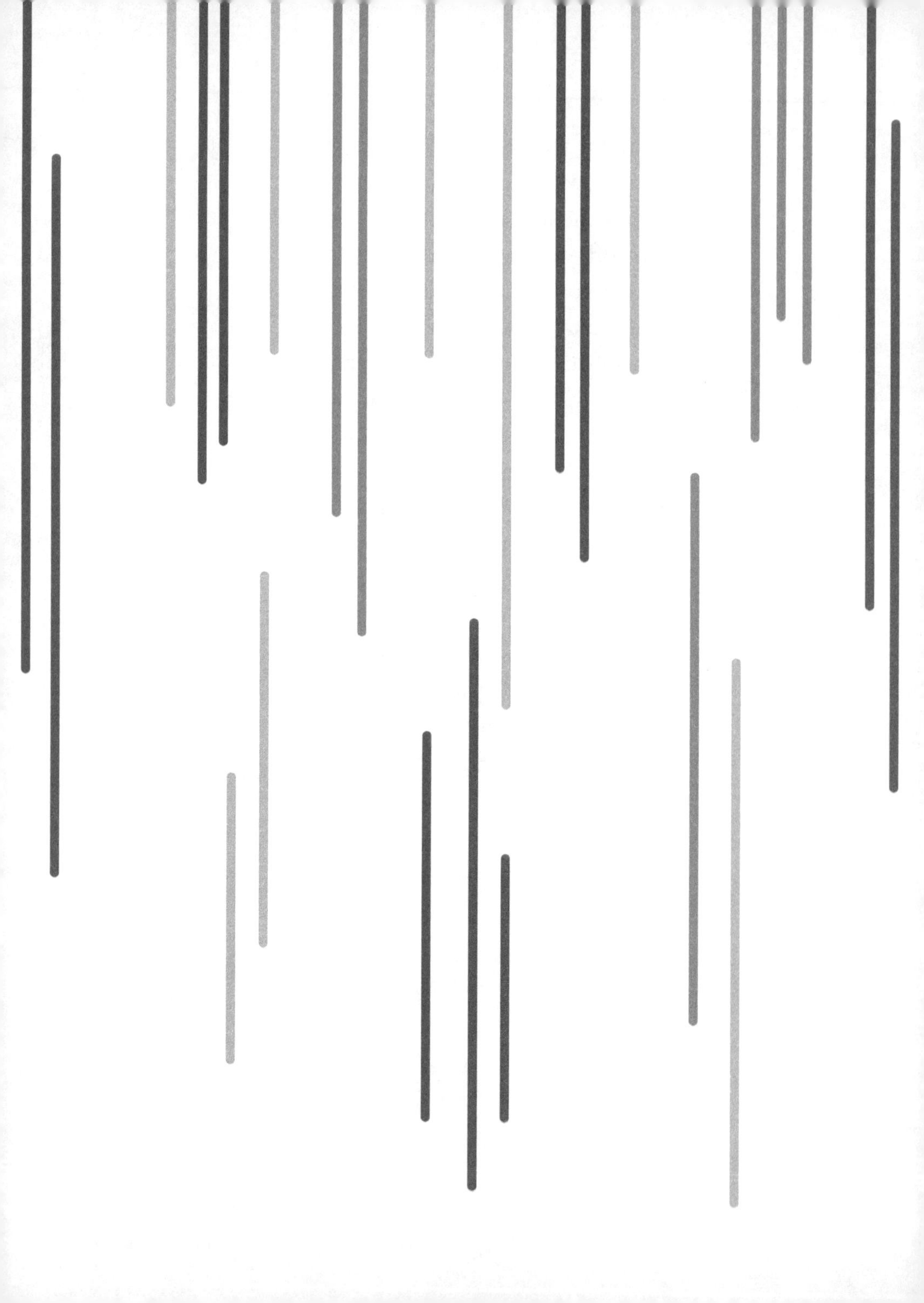

Tonight you have a skeleton in your closet, crowned with flowers, behind a thin door you know you can't lock. You read once that people long ago would compose whole messages out of bouquets, but you don't want to know what bloom your skeleton bears. You already know. It is no mummy brought on by a curse. It is the bringer. There is a secret in your closet wreathed in jonquils and tulips and it longs to close its bony fingers around your throat. If you lie very still, you think, no one will open the door. If you pretend to be asleep, it will never come out. If you play dead as a withered rose, no one ever has to know.

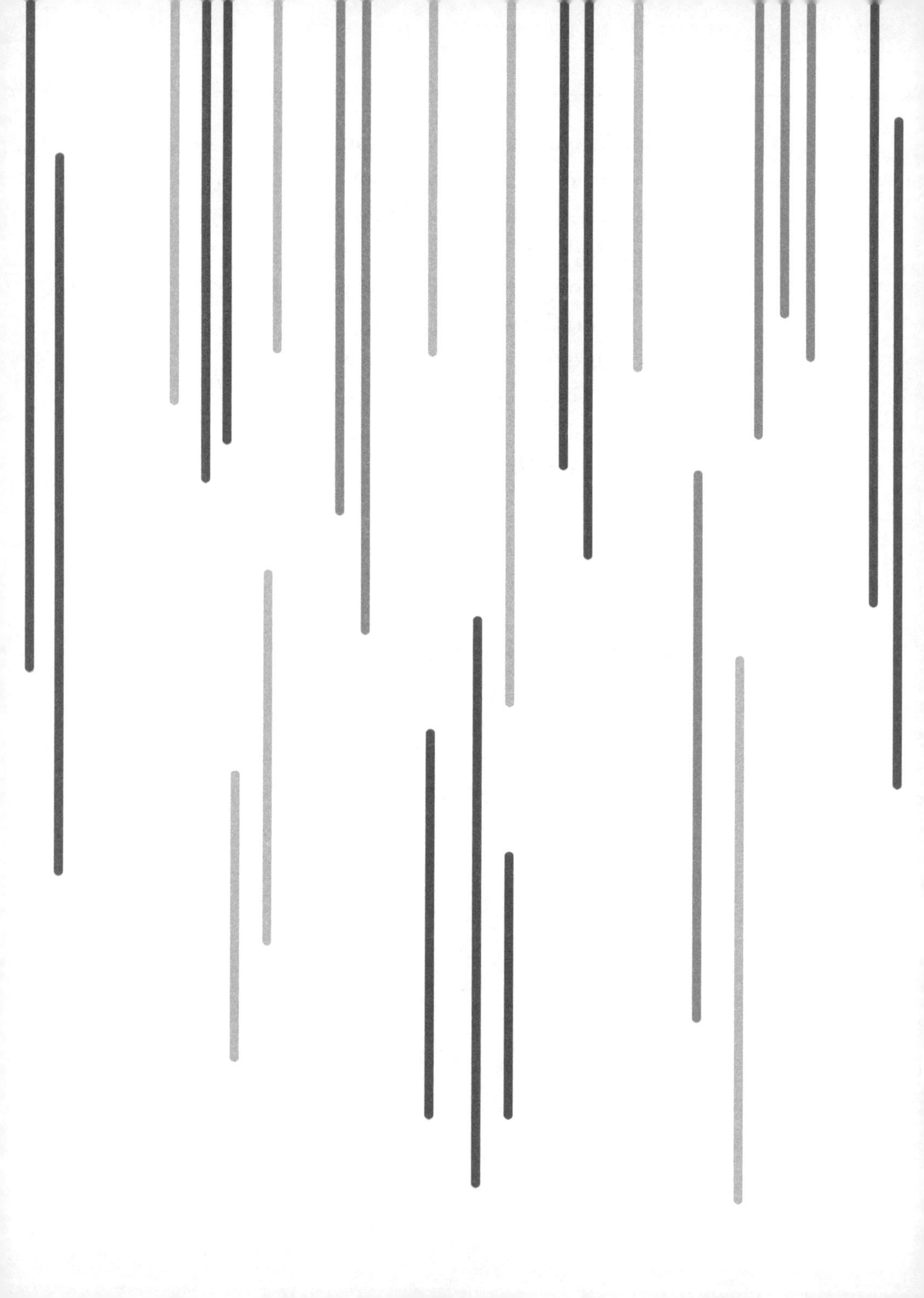

Tonight you are stamping a manifesto into a wheat field. You press down the stalks with a strange device, consult a map you've made but never actually see. You are your own labyrinth, are the minotaur chasing its shadow. You are the string and Theseus. You are sailing through the flora, a ship with black sails. *Surely the important ones will see*, you think. You are in a plane flying over flyover country, looking out the window. Down below are crop circles. You are the alien for whom they are meant. Your belief is a sword's edge, and surely those who tell you both sides can cut are the authors of some insidious hoax.

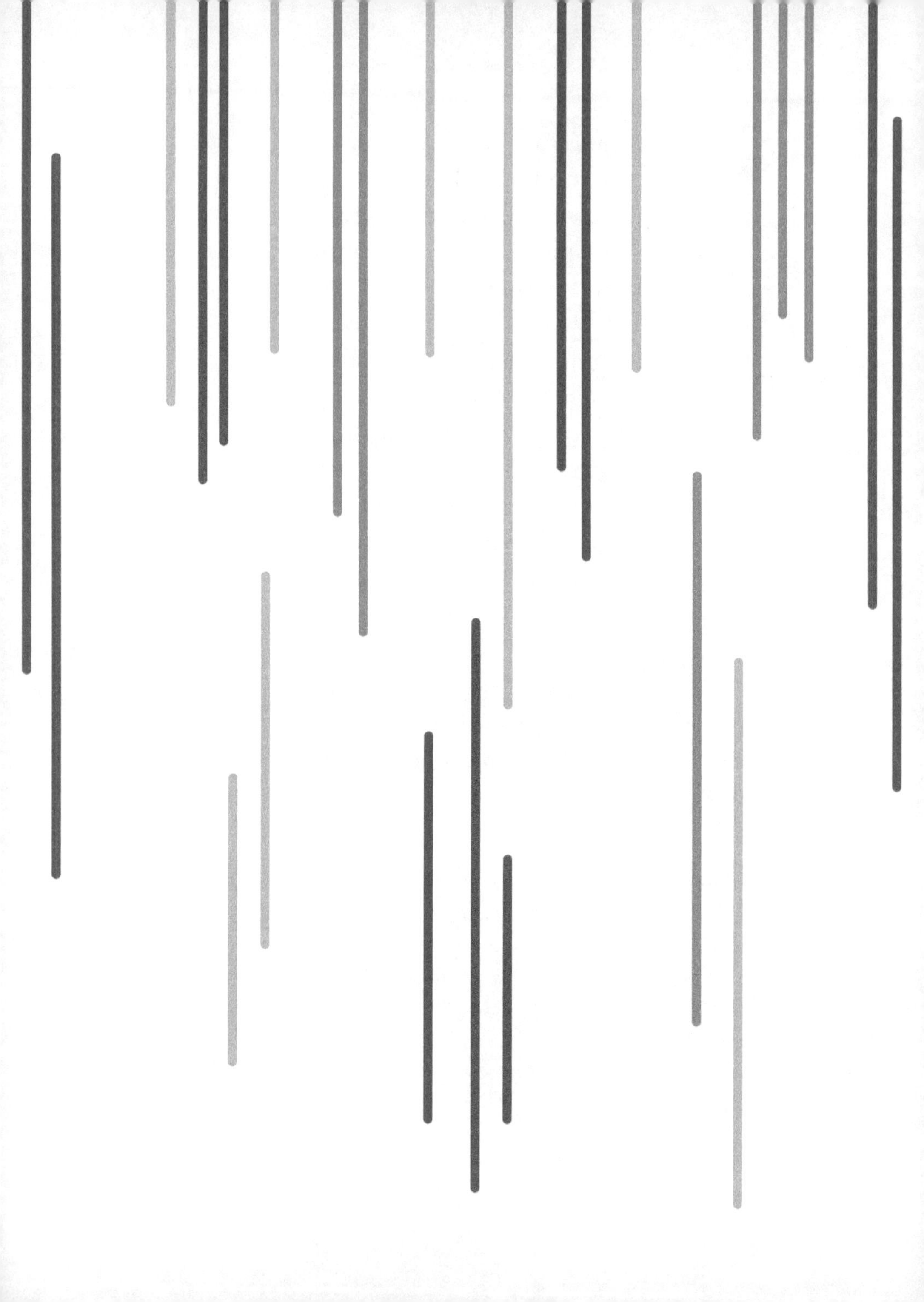

Tonight you are a confused werewolf howling at the sun. Your too-human lips purse, project inadequacy at a pitch that carries for yards instead of miles. Neighborhood dogs don't fear you. The neighbors themselves are making phone calls behind closed doors. You hear sirens later than you'd like, can't lope fast enough after or away from them. A man in a uniform barks at you. Twelve hours either direction and his innards would be your feast. As it stands, the only blood you can smell is your own.

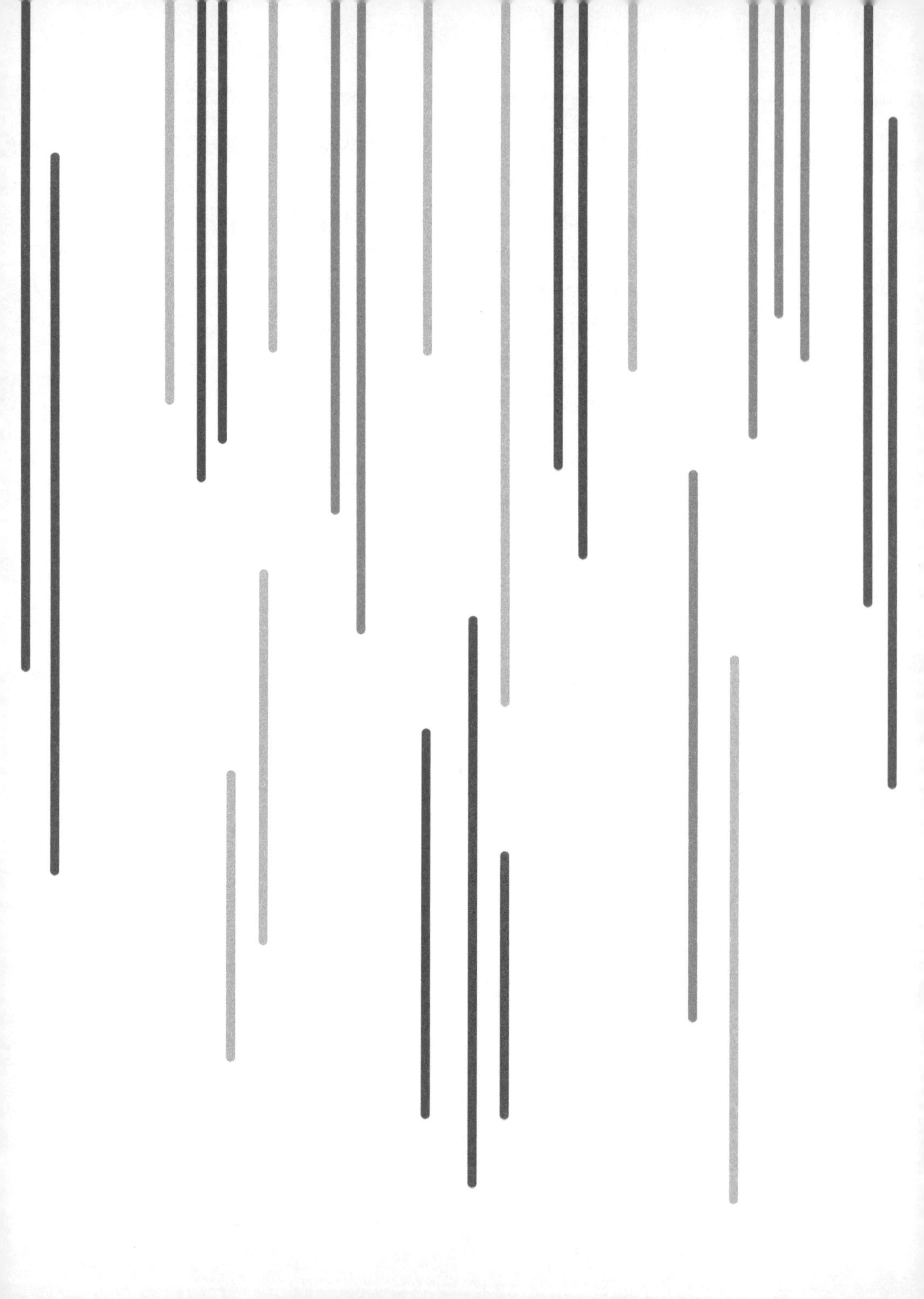

Tonight you have teeth growing out of your teeth. You're looking in the bathroom mirror as an incisor slowly protrudes from your incisor. You can feel your molars multiplying. They're beginning to grind against each other. They're beginning to slice open your mouth from the inside out. The teeth growing from your teeth are beginning to grow teeth. Your jaw is forced wide. You are full of teeth, from your guts to your fingernails. You are teeth forcing their way out of themselves. You are trying to stay calm. You can't call for help because your voice is the scraping of enamel against itself. You tell yourself it's just a dream, but then, isn't that what you said when they found the lump.

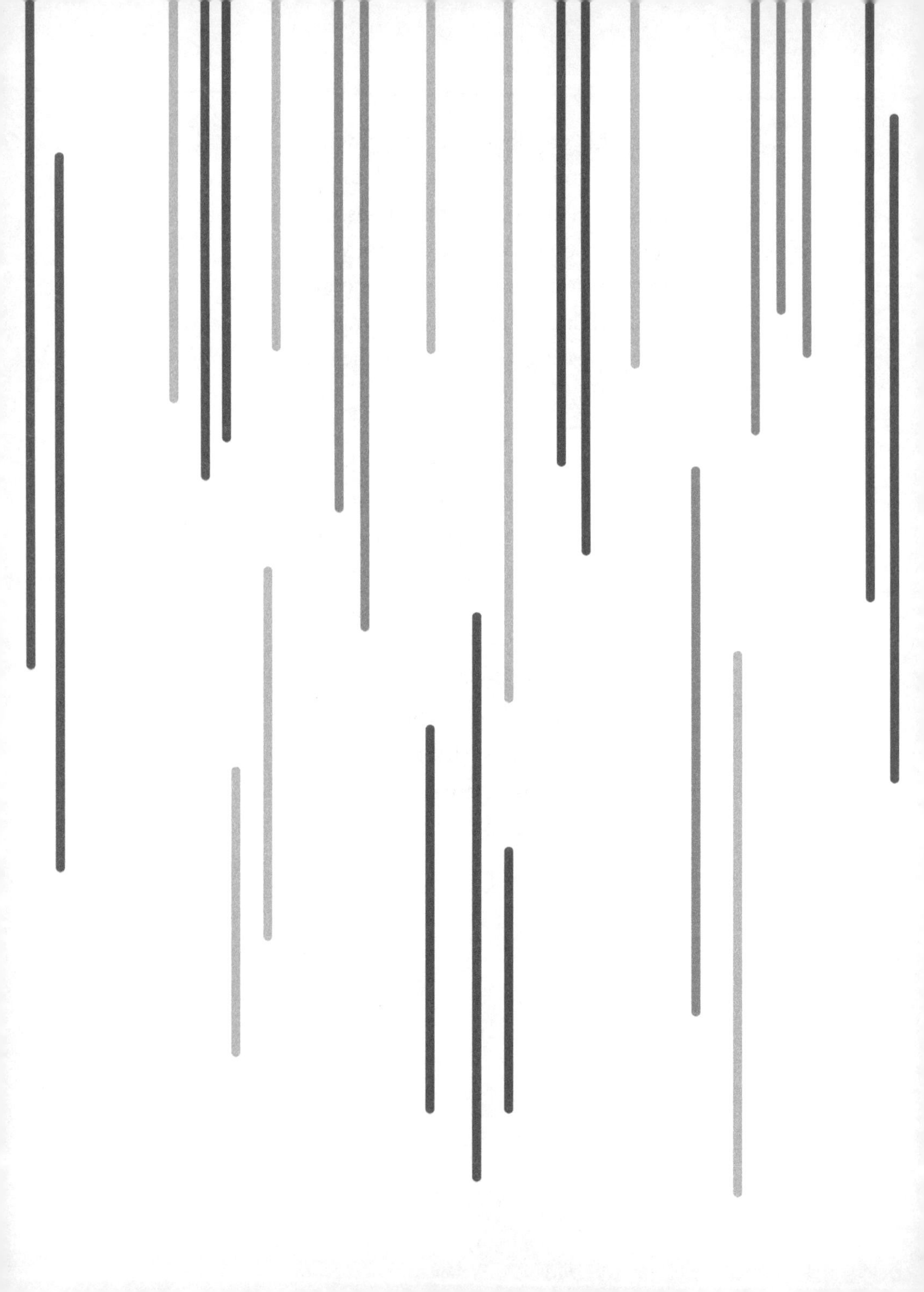

Tonight you are in a little rowboat a hundred yards offshore, and the shore is lined with women. They walk, not in unison, but as one nonetheless, into the water. Some hike up their pant legs and dresses, some don't have the energy to do anything but shamble forward. They each of them have a chain linked to one ankle, and the chains are attached at the other end to the beach. They walk into the ocean, their heads just above the water, and you know what's coming and you start to row, but the tide is coming in too quick and too red, the water rising to chins, to lips, to salt-stung eyes. You are rowing and going nowhere and the women are drowned like innocents accused of witchcraft, and you in your boat begin to sink. The beach is full of taut chains. Your mother taught you wading was dangerous, but you never imagined the tide would ever prove her right.

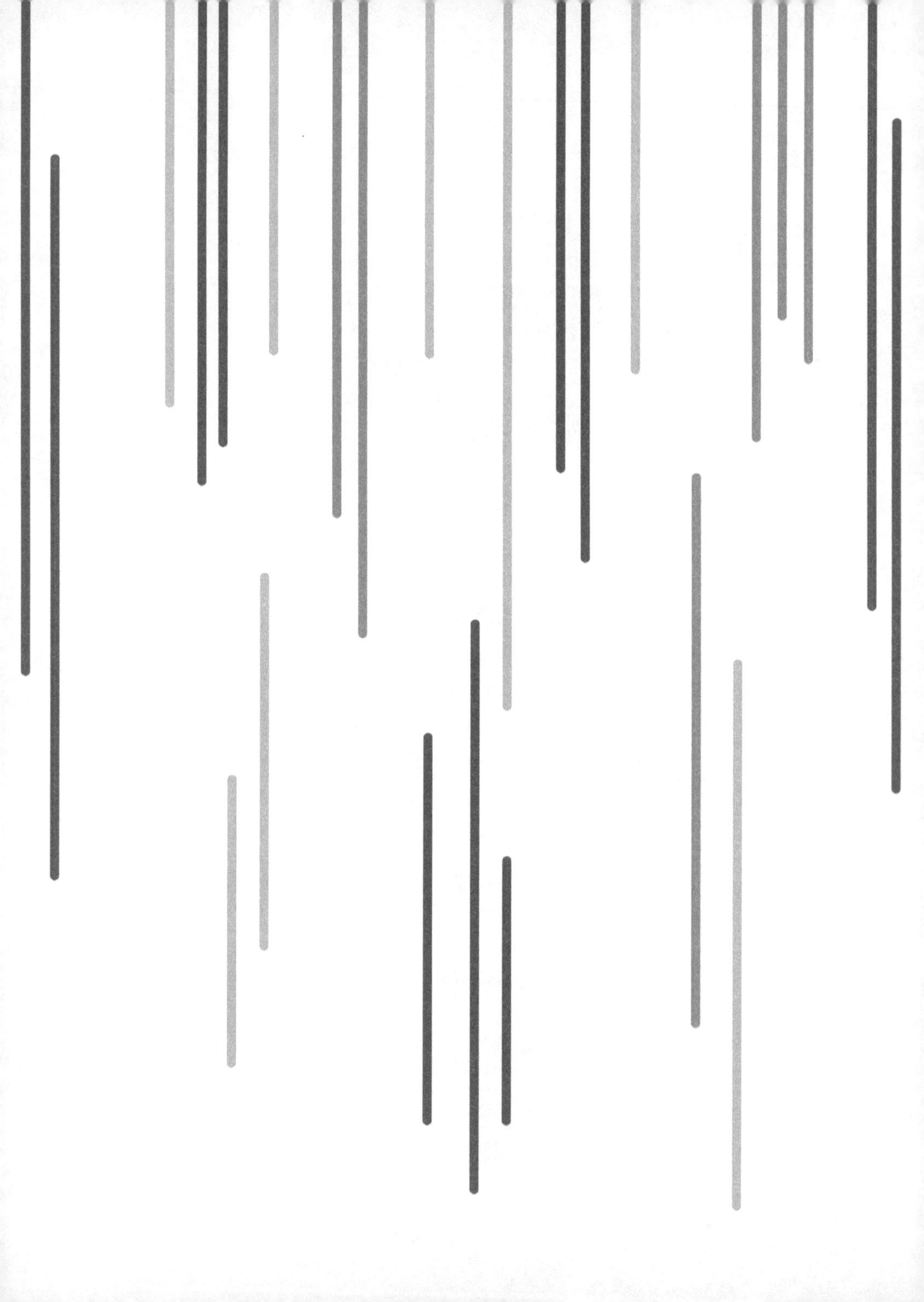

Tonight you are doing some soul searching, plunging your two good hands through the flesh of your chest, through your breastbone, gripping your ribs and prying apart the cage. You pull out your heart, hold it, listen. You rip a lung from its hangar, inspect, tear the other one loose. You hollow your torso in pursuit of something that will prove you saved, dive into your own gaping cave, a small you swimming down through your own blood. Somewhere you know there has to be a thing that will loose you from this world, grant passage. You'll destroy all of you to find it.

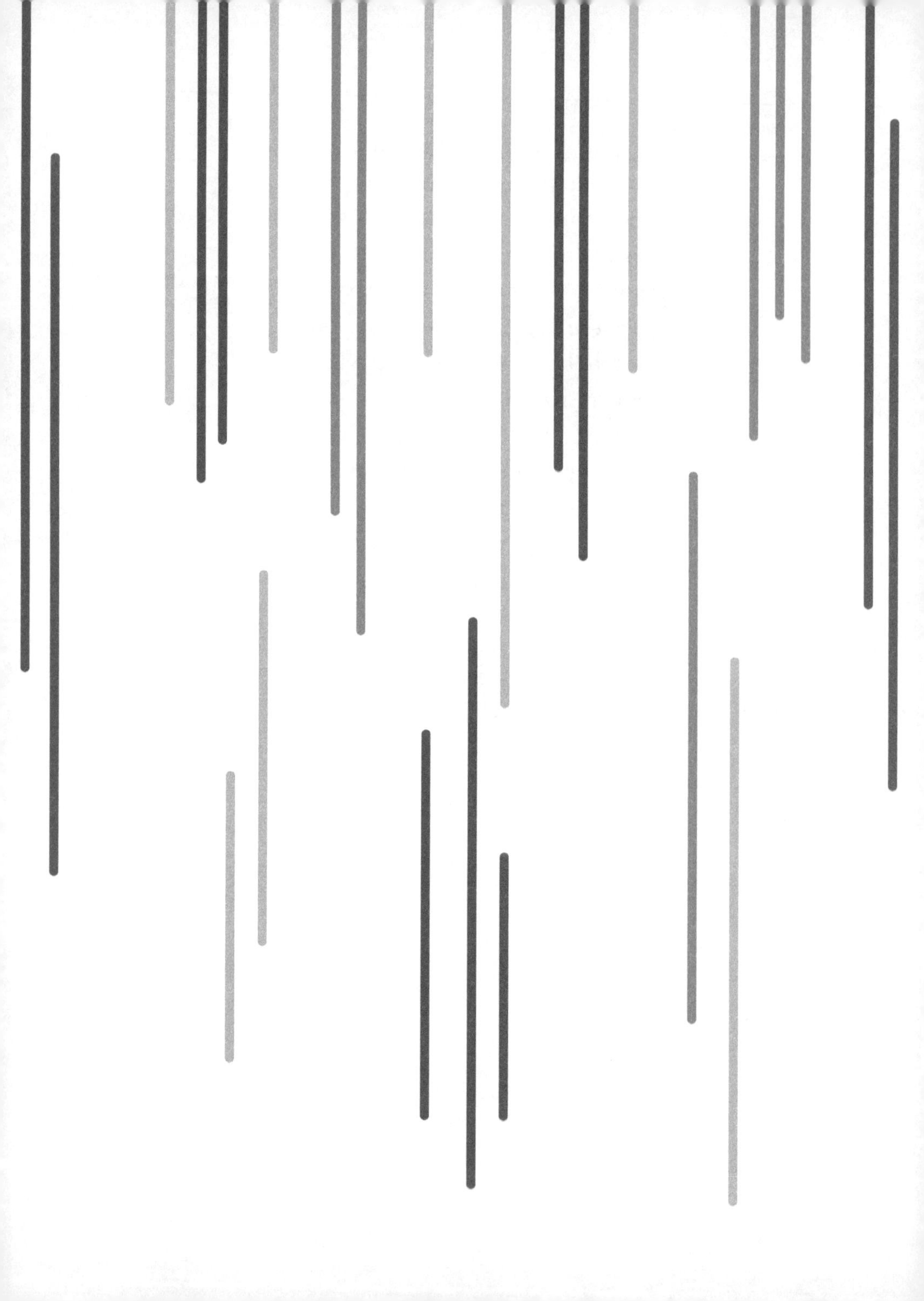

Tonight you are famous and naked. You can't look down, the way a pig can't look up, but you know you're wearing nothing but the guitar slung around your neck. Somehow the audience doesn't realize so long as you can start singing soon. You can't sing. The words were stolen by the albatross. You back into the drums, and the drummer mistakes it for a cue. You are awkward. They mistake it for swaggering indifference. This was a mistake. You don't know how you got here. A bottle falls, breaks, The Big Bang. The drummer hesitates, the audience buzzes, but you suddenly know the words. You won't remember them when you wake. If you ever wake. You're sure this is a dream. None of these people are real. That's how you know you're really famous. You are clear-throated and strong and forgetful. You are bigger than gods, the audience miles beneath you like airplanes.

Tonight you are cleaning meat crayon off the highway, by the flashing lights of your ambulance. The cop on site intones, *donorcycle*, and the word echoes heavily. You start looking for organs, find an intact lung, lift it, see an esophagus and tongue come with it. When you squeeze, it makes a noise like a drunkard cheering. *It's not the worst you've seen*, you think. You remember every crash at once, and there they are, stretching down the illuminated road: *red, white, red, white, red, white.*

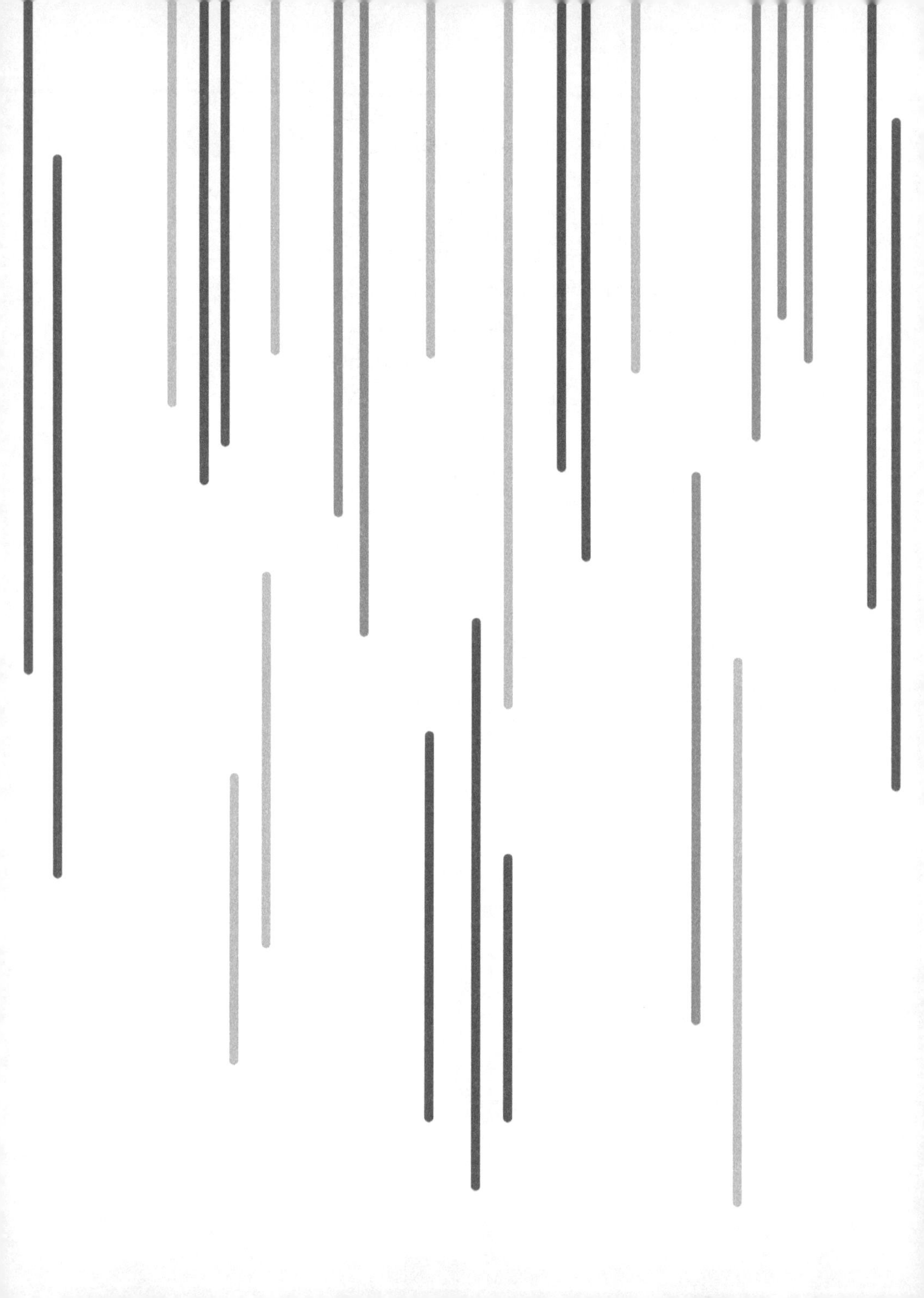

Tonight you are late at the office, trying to finish the quarterly report. Even the janitor has left by now. You keep thinking you see Gary out of the corner of your eye. In the fluorescent light, you're not sure what you see besides columns of numbers. You're not sure you know a Gary. You had a dream that you missed the twins' birthday. You might not have twins. You might be mistaking column H for the kids you've forgotten about. You're typing so loudly that someone could sneak up on you, and you'd never know. They're behind you, you know. Gary and the twins and the janitor. Staring. You can't look. You have to finish the quarterly report. Tomorrow is the deadline. You make yourself not say that word. You giggle a bit because numbers are imaginary. If you stare at the screen without blinking, you barely notice the keyboard visible through your fading hands.

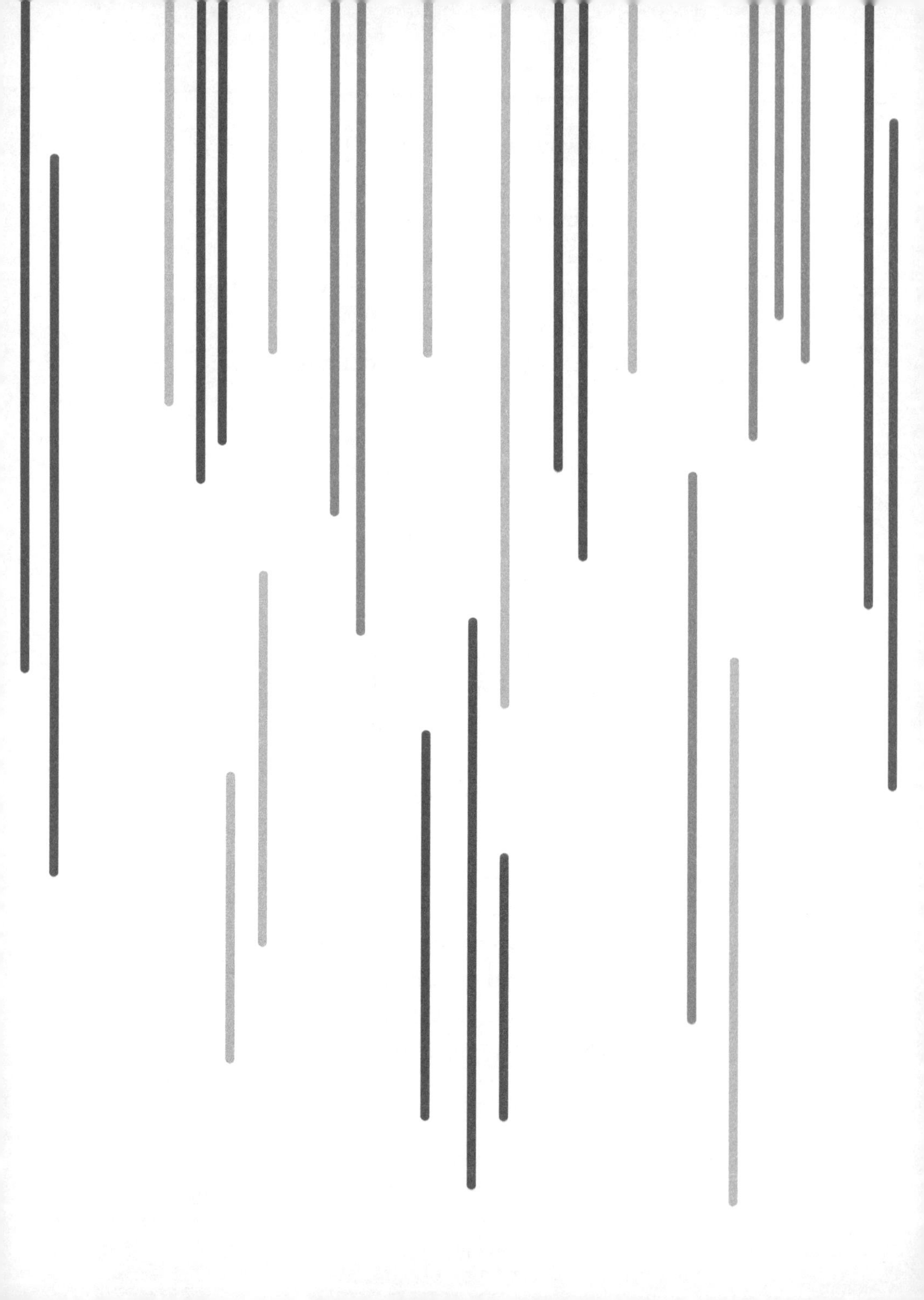

Tonight you are wascally, all wobbly limbs and optional gravity. You are free falling next to a redheaded gunslinger. You pull out a bottle of hare tonic and float safely to the forest floor. A hunter points a gun in your face, but you wrap your long ears into a turban, pull a flute out of thin air and charm him like a snake. You are your own lucky rabbit's foot. You are never in season. You can tie a shotgun in knots as easily as putting on a dress. You just exude a little confidence and twist, twist, twist.

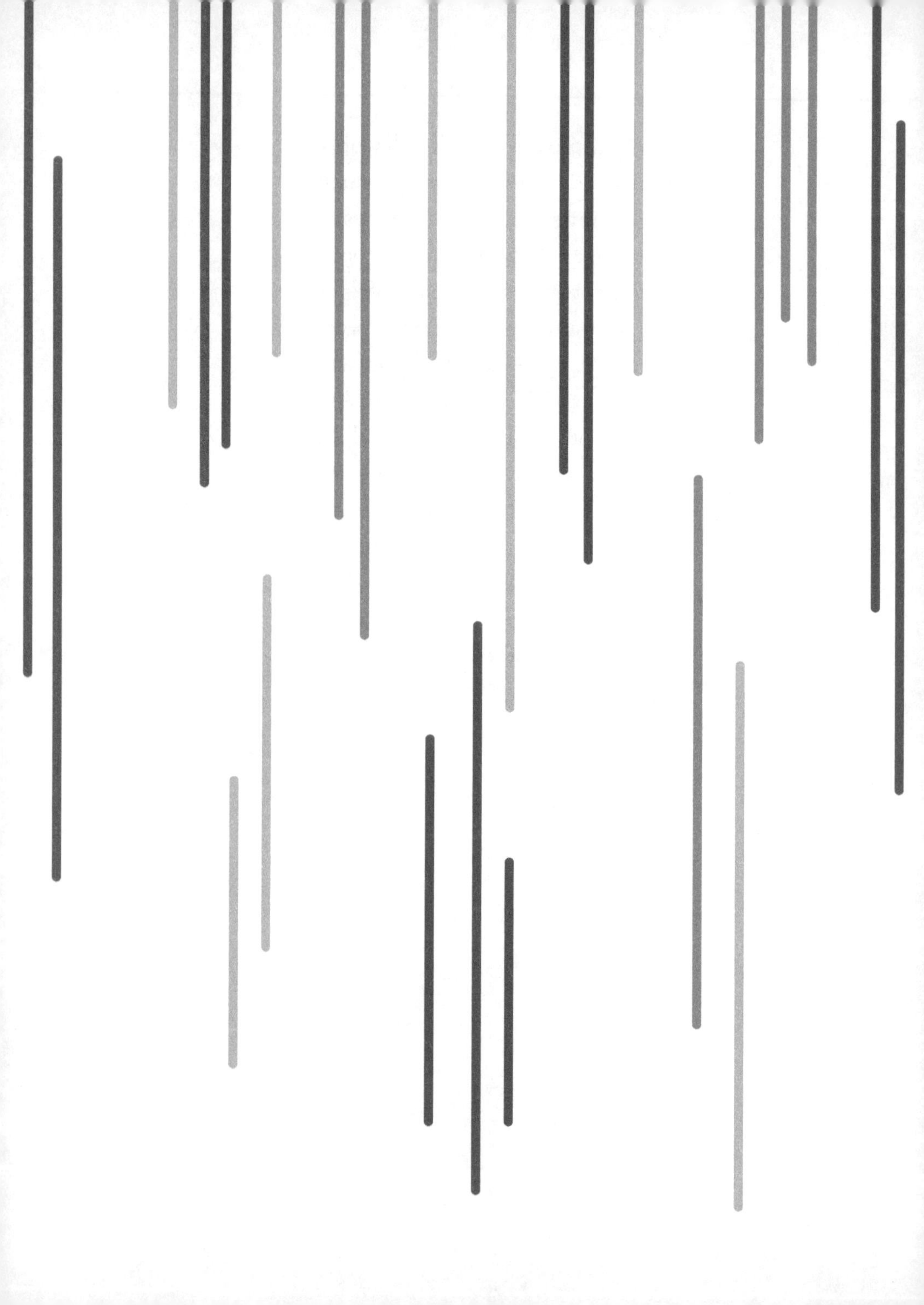

Tonight you are bagging groceries. You drop in a loaf of bread, reach for the next item, see an identical loaf of bread. You think it might be the same loaf. The bag is empty. You put the loaf in the bag, look up, see it again. The cashier is ringing up more items. The line is getting longer. You reach for something else, find a loaf of bread in your hand. You put it in the bag. The bag is empty. People are piling up on each other like they're on a conveyer belt. They're angry at you. You smash the loaf into the bag. The bag is empty. The manager is perpetually walking toward you. You are paid by the hour. Your watch flickers between now and a minute ago. Everything is moving. Nothing is changing.

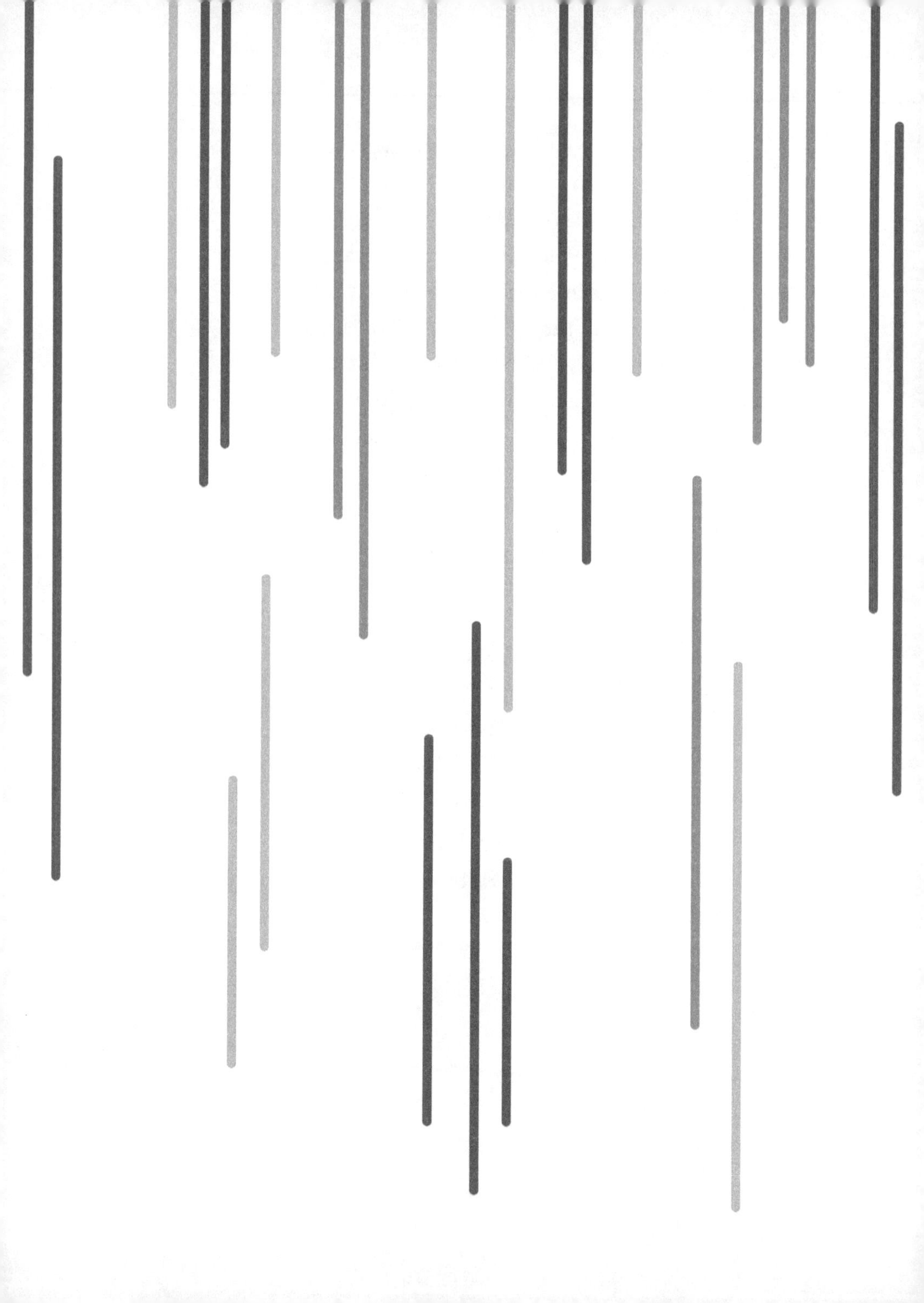

Tonight you can't keep the dogs from drowning. There is a bed on the edge of a lake, on the edge of a swamp. You're not sure. You don't have time to look up. Your dogs are here with you, on the bed on the edge of unknowable waters. The bed tips and the dogs spill off the edge. You pull them back up. The bed tips again. Over and over, over and over, Death's Own Metronome. Your arms are full of lead and regret. The dogs are heavier than loss because you're losing them. The fact that you'll soon have to choose one over another blooms in your mind like a cancer. You understand that in this place choosing means hurting, and isn't that the way of it all. Isn't that what led you here.

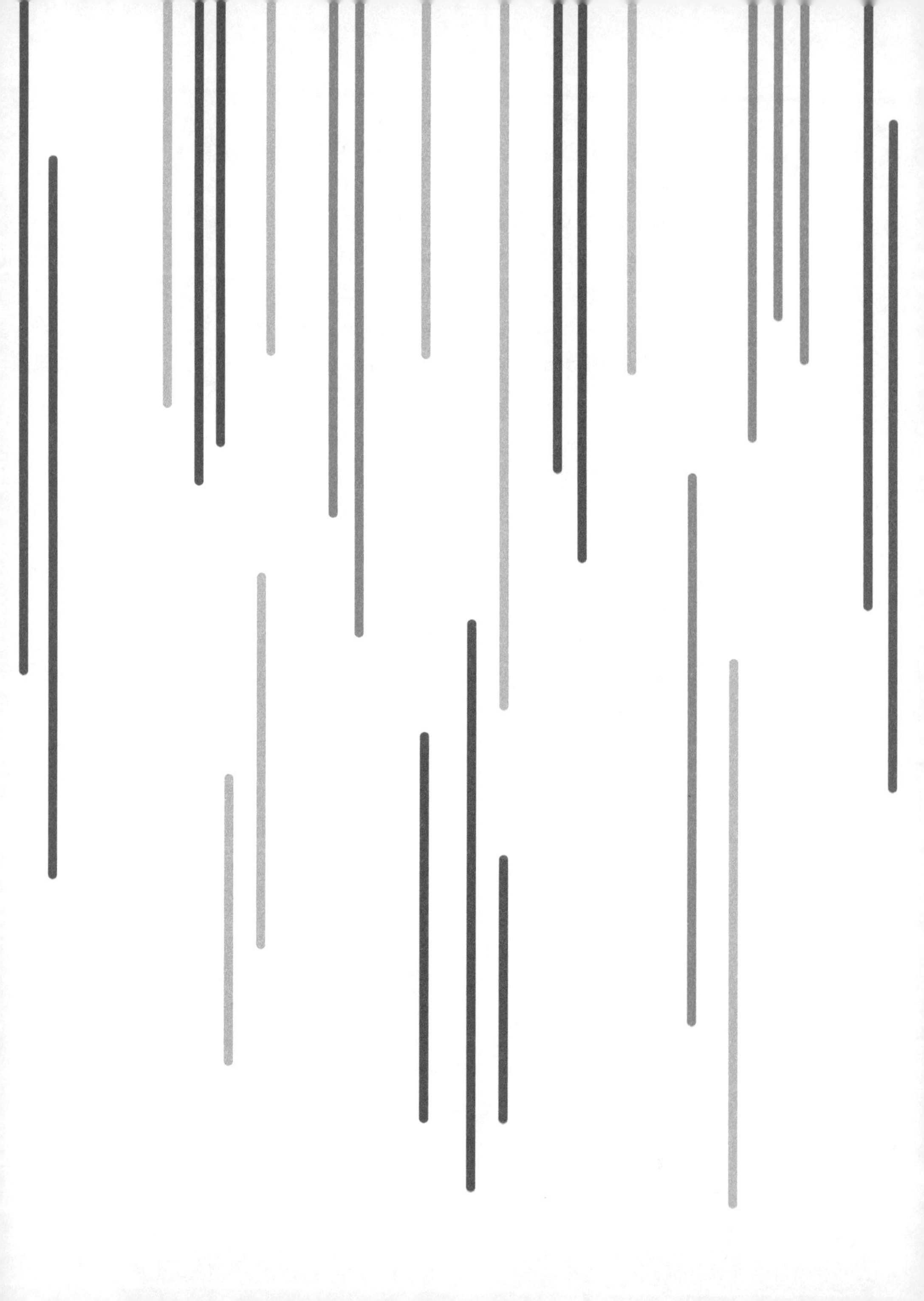

Tonight you are doing nothing wrong, and there are body parts masquerading as policemen all over 32nd Ave. There's a nose outside Tong's Restaurant and another at the hot dog cart. Three pairs of eyes walk slowly on the other side of the street. A hand is in the alley pushing a homeless guy against the wall. There are teeth and a tongue gripping a bystander's phone. A hunk of fat tall as the doorway leers at a woman passing by, averting her gaze from the world. You are pressing yourself into the bricks as if you can press yourself into the bricks. You are doing nothing wrong. You are doing nothing wrong. You can't press hard enough. What a curse is flesh.

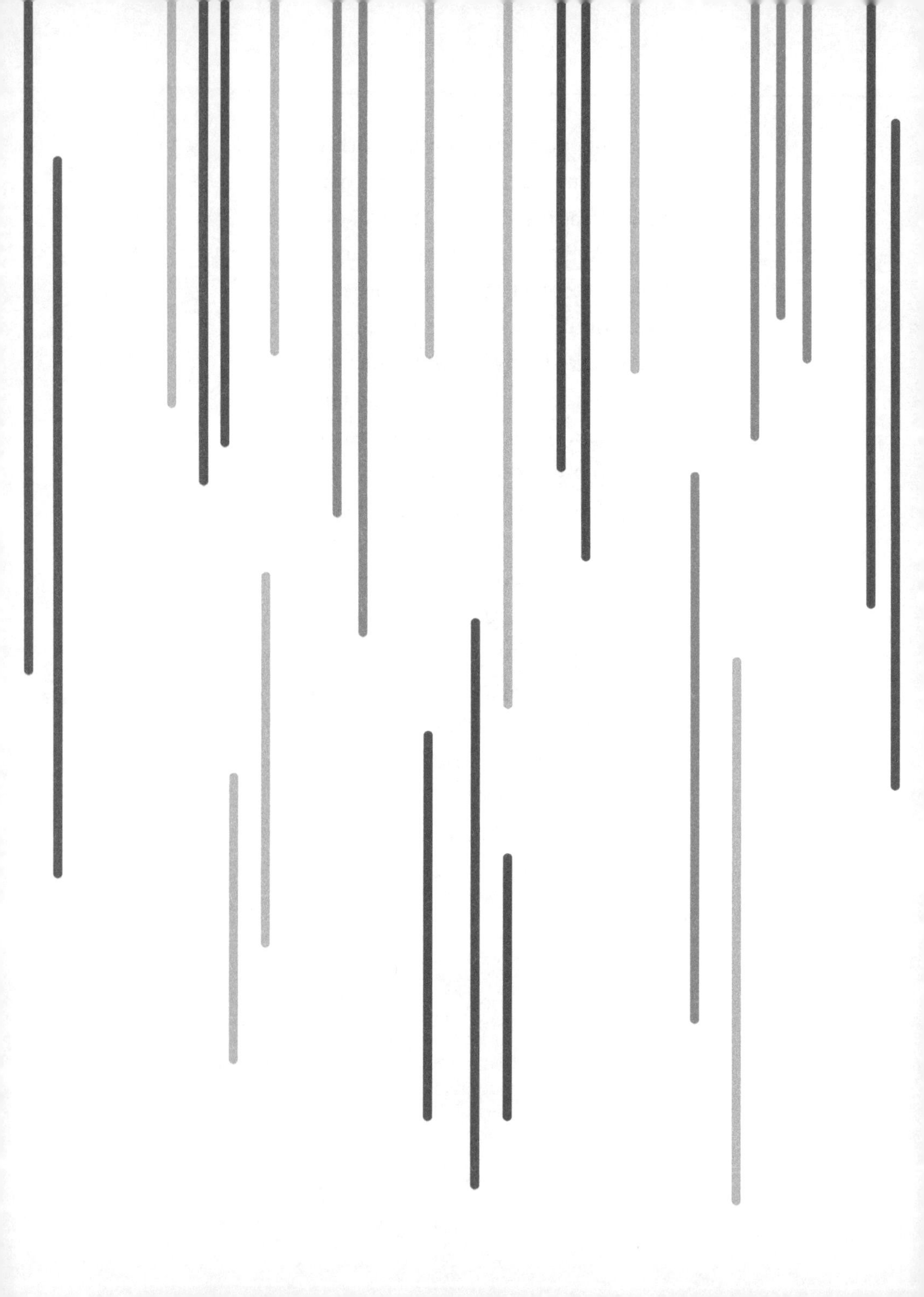

Tonight you are a security camera panning across a small room. The room is filled with vivisected bodies. You don't know how they got here. You don't know who they are. You don't. You can't stop looking. You are an unlubricated eye. The bodies. You can't tell how deeply they're piled. They go down forever. The small room is a well. It is a room. There are four walls and you and the bodies. You want to find meaning. No. You want to stop looking. You are a security camera panning. You want to stop looking. You are Panopticon. You want. When all you have is an eye, everything looks like a spectacle.

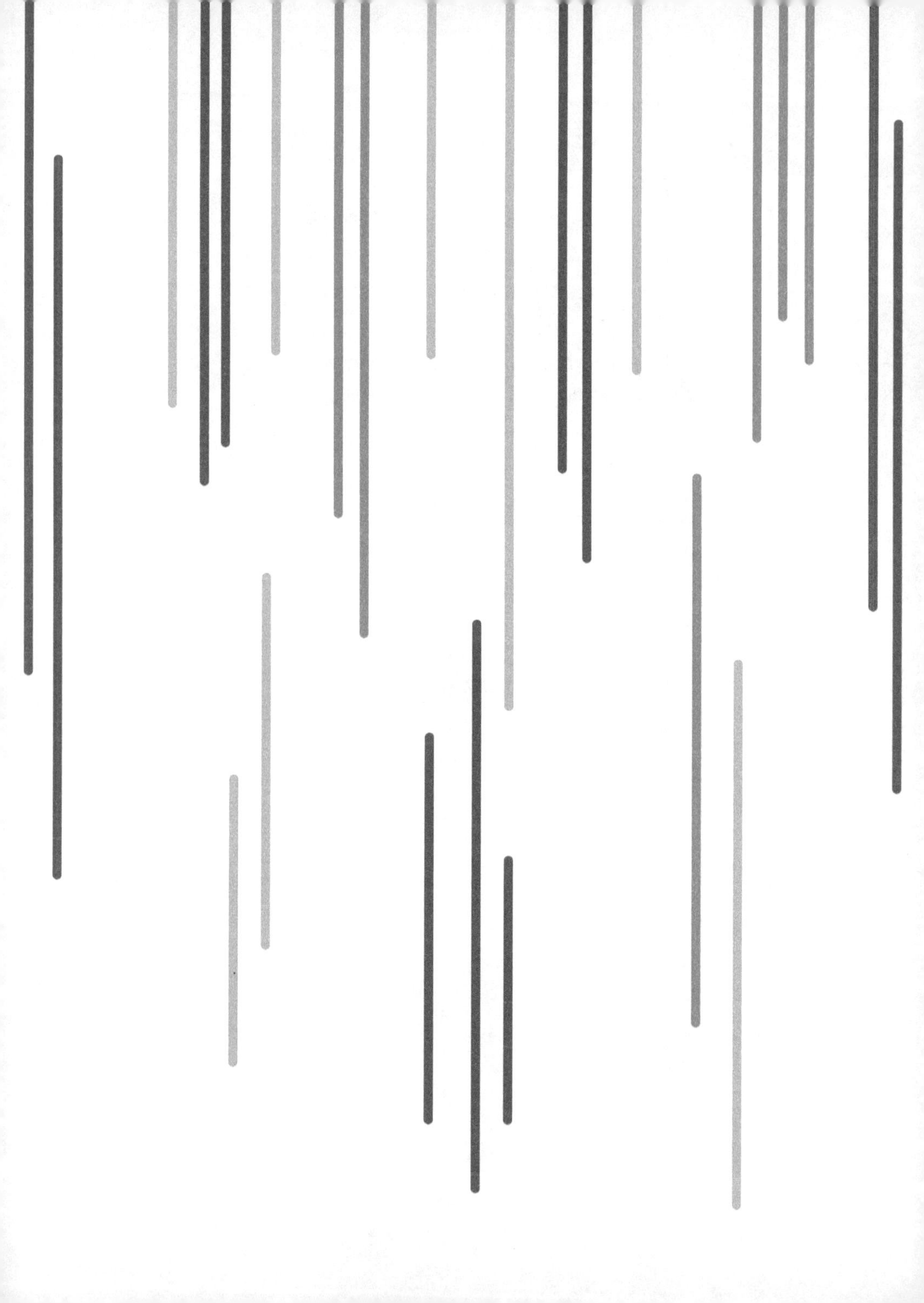

Tonight you are a watch face spinning like a gyroscope. You are a glass sphere, an electron shell. You are a grandfather paradox clock. You aren't sure you even exist now. You are Big Ben mid-explosion, your giant hands frozen in flight over the Thames. You are a dangerous landmark. The old folks say a stopped clock is still right twice a day, but they've never seen anything as broken as you.

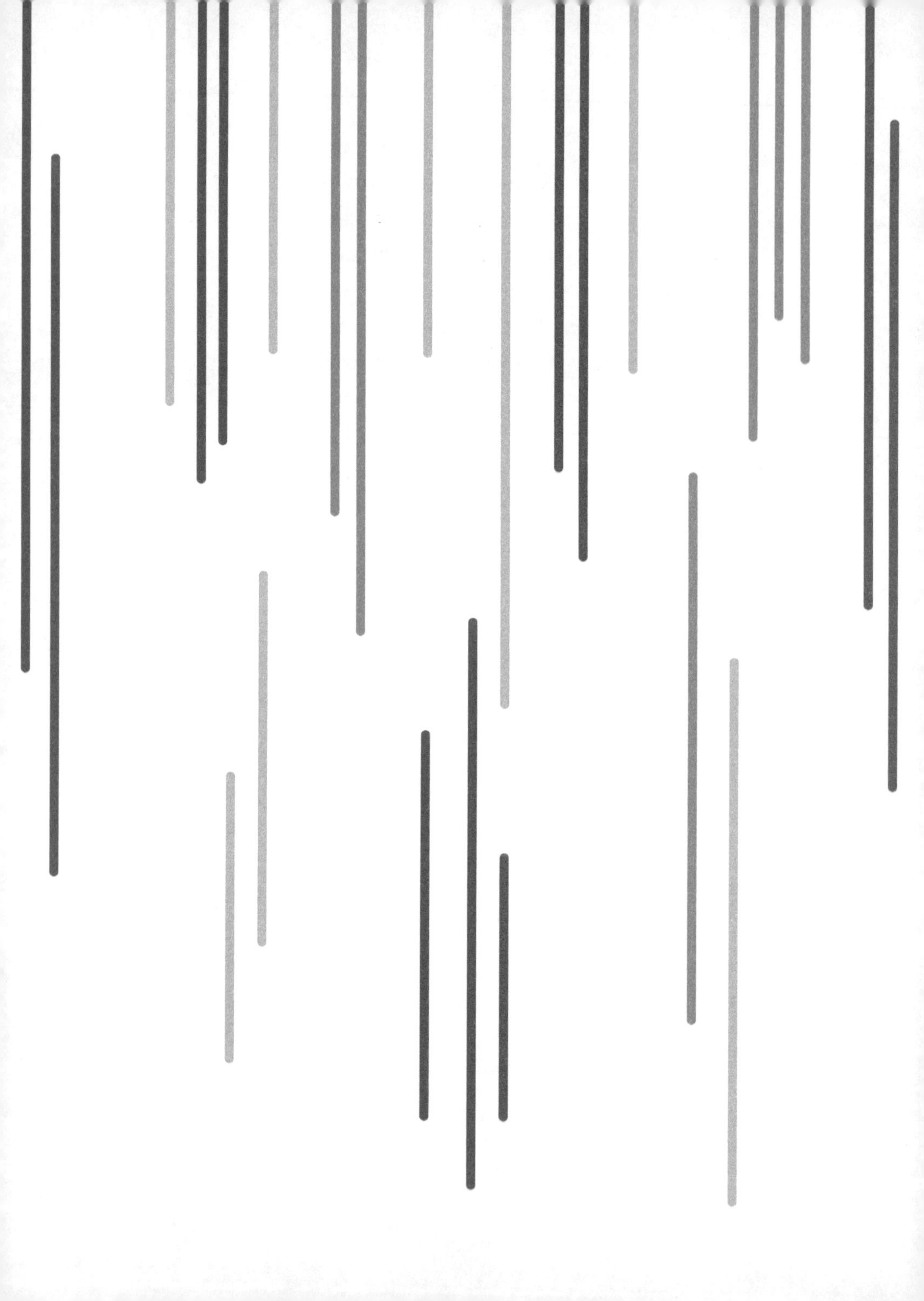

Tonight you are poking at roadkill with a pronged stick. It is a sparrow, a hawk, an eagle, smashed flat against the asphalt but for one upturned wing. You are suddenly small as an ant, gazing up, covered in shadow and foreshadow. You are yourself. It is high noon in the Old West. You turn over the stick and get blood on your claws. You are not a killer. You are a carrion bird. *Death is the only currency here,* says the corpse. There are maggots on its eyes like coins you can't spend. The curse of the bird god echoes in your tiny brain: *Because you have betrayed my trust, you will only find water that belongs to another. It will be their blood. Drink, and remember me.*

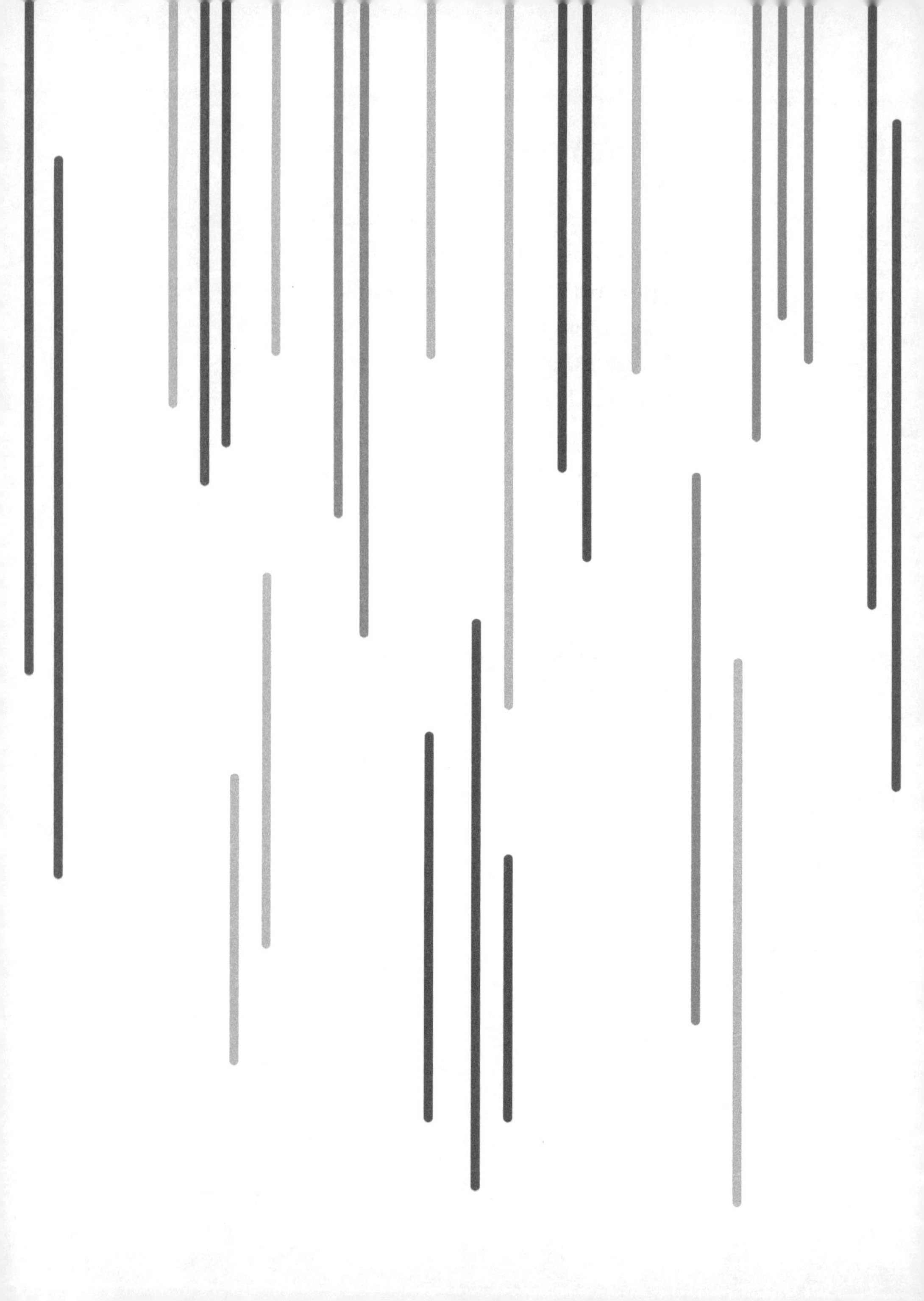

Tonight you are palming glass stones. Your house is glass and you must defend it. Your neighbor is pulling back a glass slingshot. You are steadying a glass handgun. Your neighbor is aiming a glass cannon. Your glass tank is rumbling onto the yard. Your neighbor's house is a glass aircraft carrier. You are making a call on a glass phone and sirens break the air. The Earth hangs in space like an ornament, shatters into a trillion nothingnesses. You zoom backward past a glass solar system, crushed moons in your wake. You hope you will find a new home. You trail galaxies from your arms.

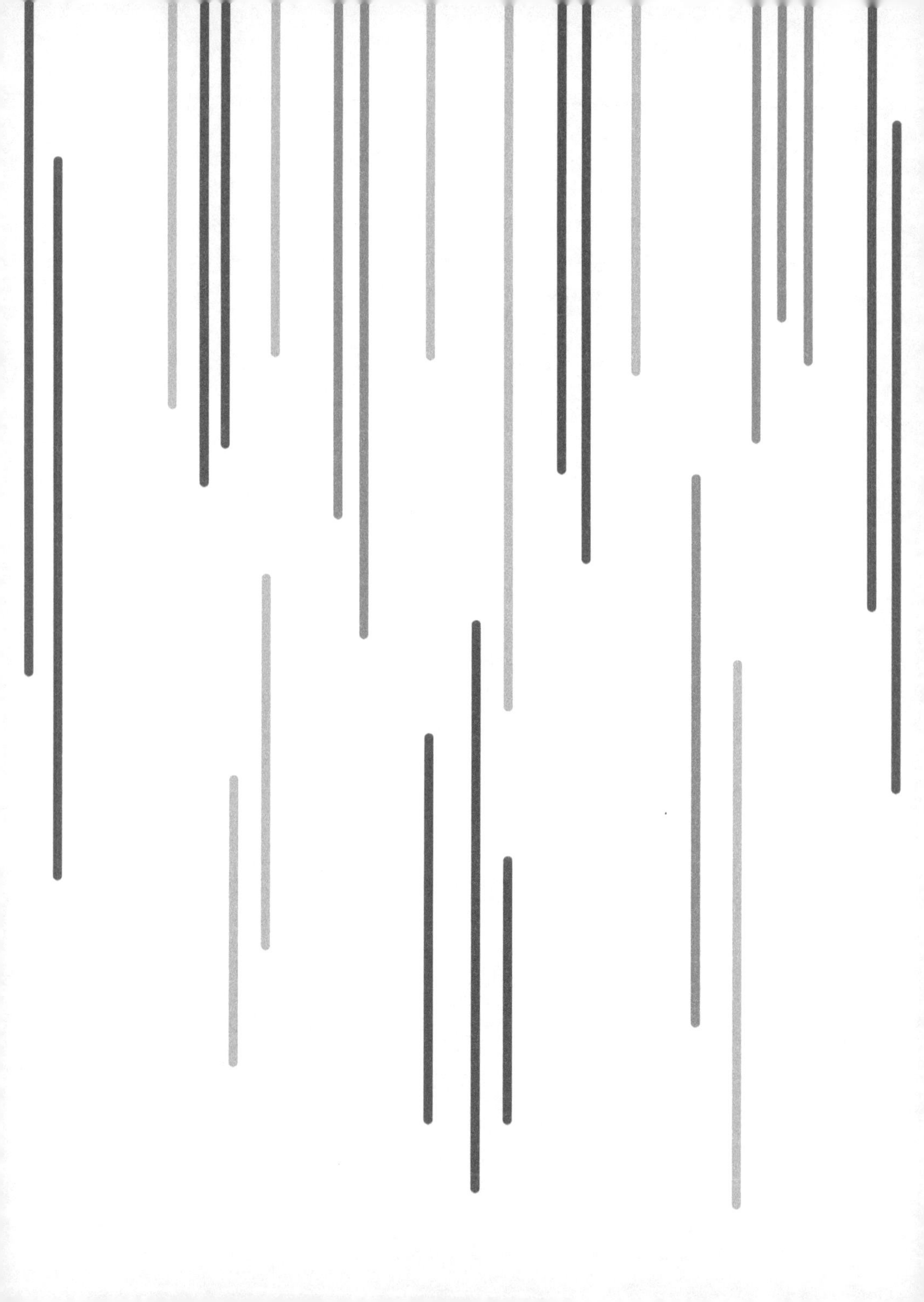

Tonight you are not the sailor but the shipwreck, your huge hull split and creaking. Downpour. Lightning. You think in a former life you were the haft of a spear of a man guarding Atlantis. Perhaps that's what brought you back to the sea, disparate timbers chasing someone else's purpose. But it's down there, somewhere, far, far down, and it is calling with its rusty bells. You are bloodless and broken on an outcropping of rock. The captain steered you wrong, then abandoned you to the storm. Atlantis sank for hubris. You had no ego when you cut the waters. You thought this Nirvana. But your lot seems to be paying for some human's sins. Tonight is for the dark and the dying, if a ship be ever alive. Tonight is for the memories carried beneath decks, sunk beneath waves. Tonight you are afraid to go sleep, as if it is your choice. Who knows if you will wake up too far from the ocean. Who knows if any hand will hold and guide you back.

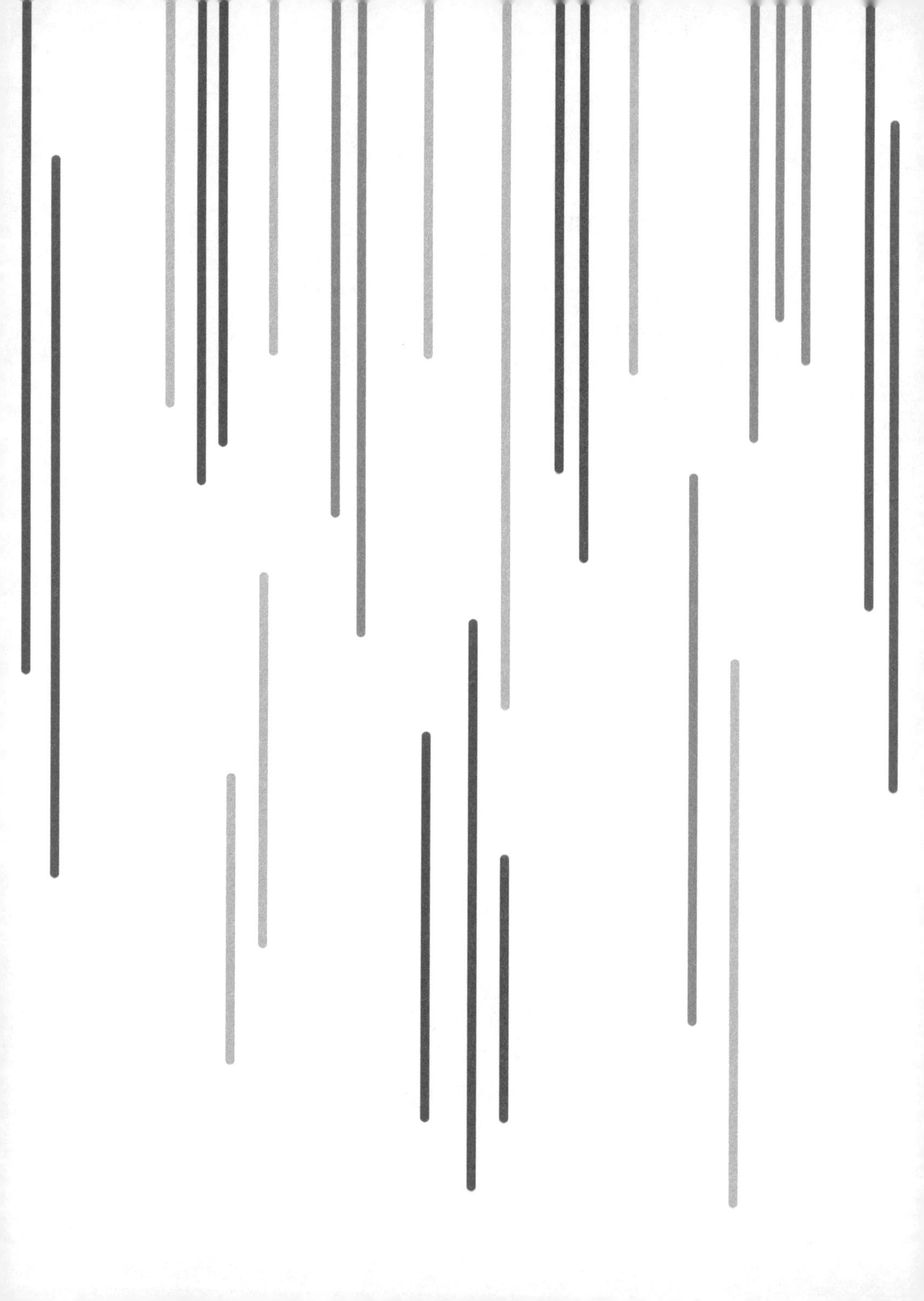

Tonight you are trying to turn the TV down. The newscasters are drowning out your thoughts. You press the volume down button, and the volume turns up. You do it again, and your eardrums burst. You try another button, another, another. You are jamming your fingers on the remote, slamming your hand on it. You throw it at the TV with all your strength, and the screen splinters into a hundred-headed pundit. The news is a screaming hydra. It's so loud it's beyond sound. There are hydras in your teeth, breaking them from the inside out. You can feel your skull splitting like a screen, soon to birth a hundred talking heads.

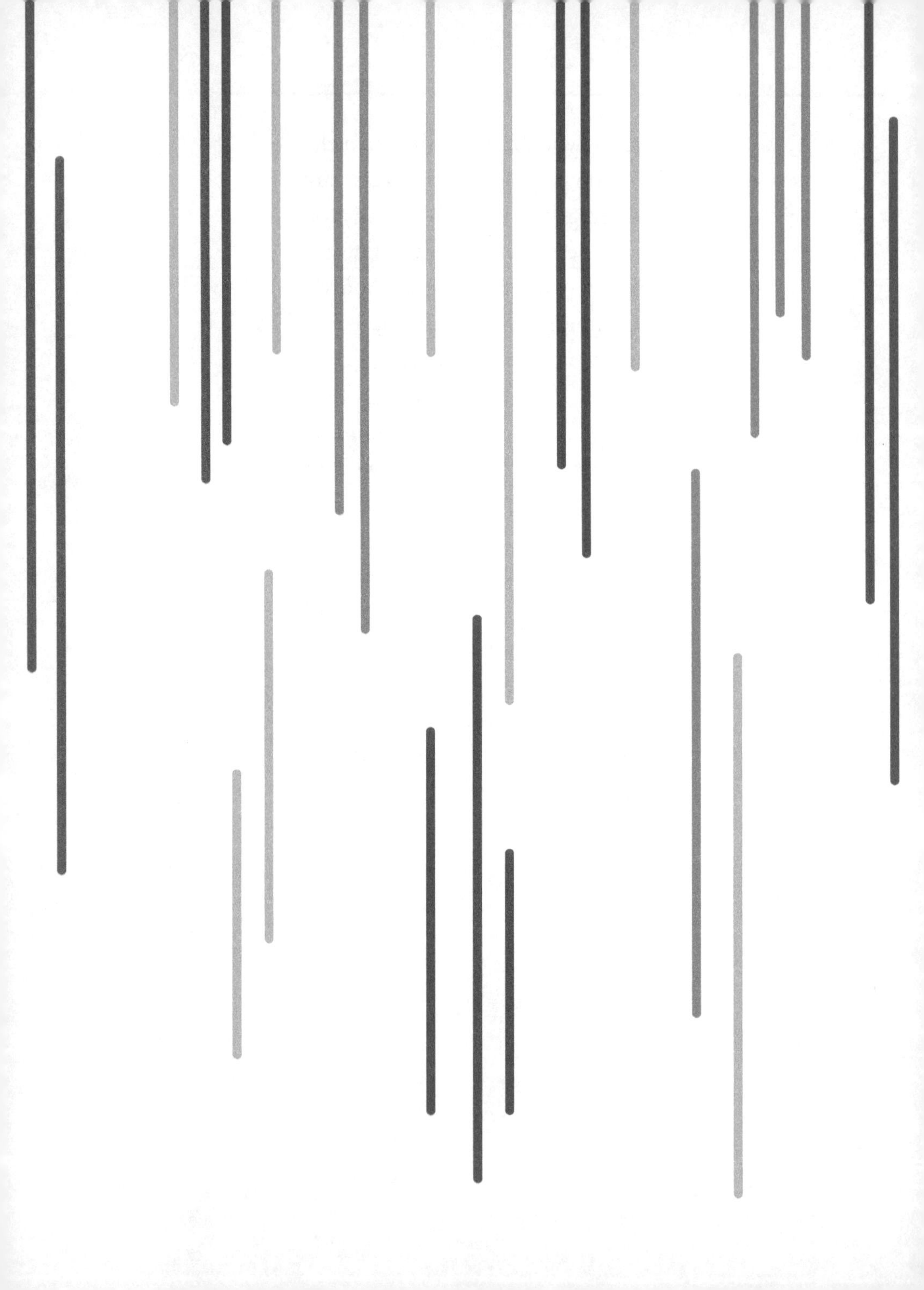

Tonight you are picking out what to wear to Solomon's palace. Nothing too expensive; he won't believe you need help. Nothing too cheap; you won't be seen. You dye your wedding veil black in a scrying bowl, walk out the door otherwise nude. When you arrive, the Other Mother is already there with your baby. In your mind's eye, you are clawing your child out of her arms. In the palace, you are cool as a bust. You enter side-by-side, present the baby, ask for judgment/justice. Solomon bids his guard divide the child, to each of you a half. You cry do/do not, and he says, *Give it to the one who would not have it die*, but your heart is already in twain on the floor. You split yourself bringing it into the world. You split yourself to care for it. You split yourself to save it from you.

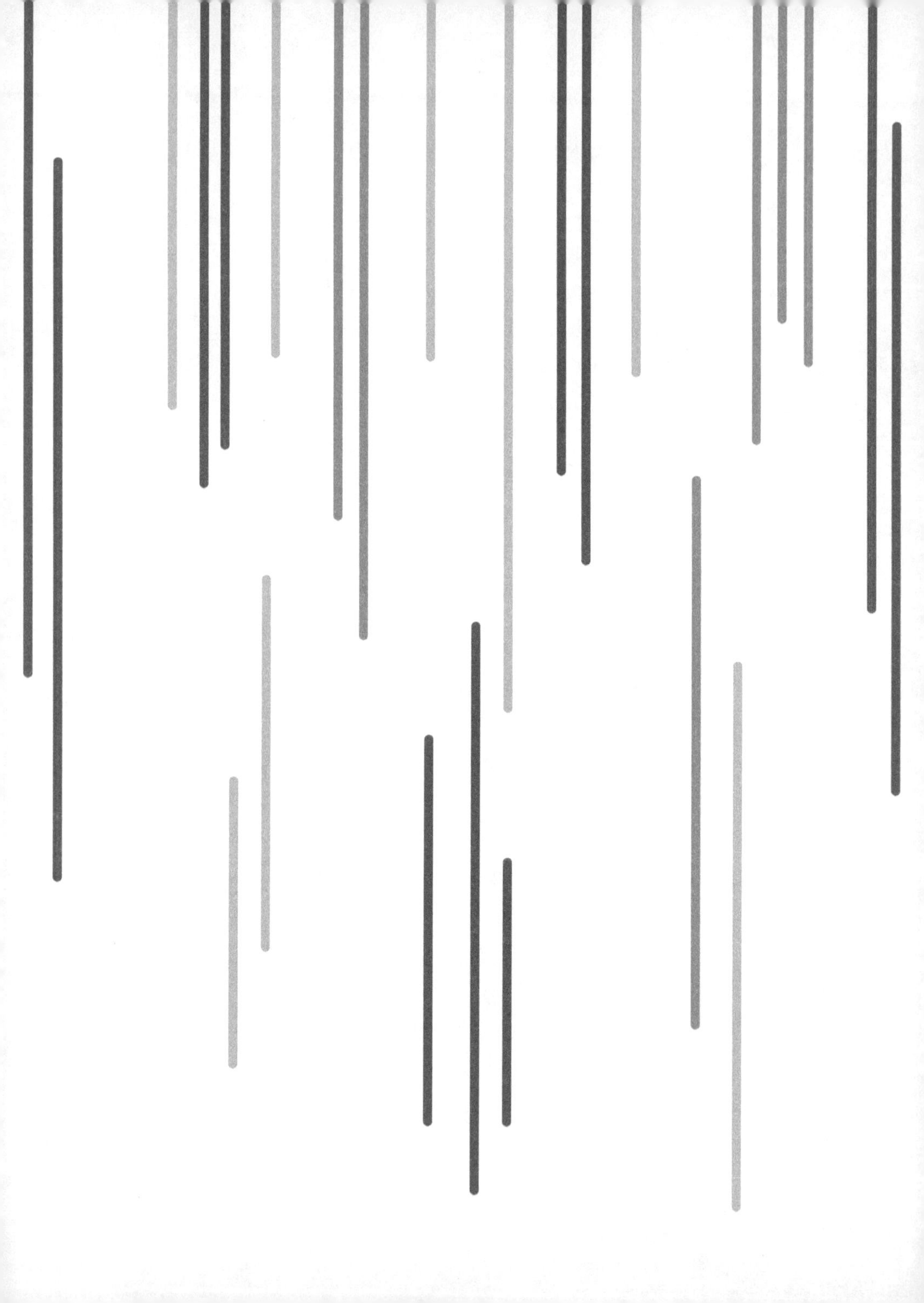

Tonight you are in front of your first-grade classroom. You are not sure what you are presenting. You are not presenting. You are the presentation. The teacher cuts off the top of your skull with a sharp blade and lifts it off. She holds up a mirror so that you can see. Your brain is nine small globes orbiting a tenth like the solar system. She holds up a planet to show the class, and it slips through her fingers and splatters on the floor. She does it again. She does it again. All your precious brains spilled, busted open like ripe fruit. You want to say something, but it's hard to comprehend what is happening, let alone open your tiny dribbling mouth and whisper to authority, *Why?*

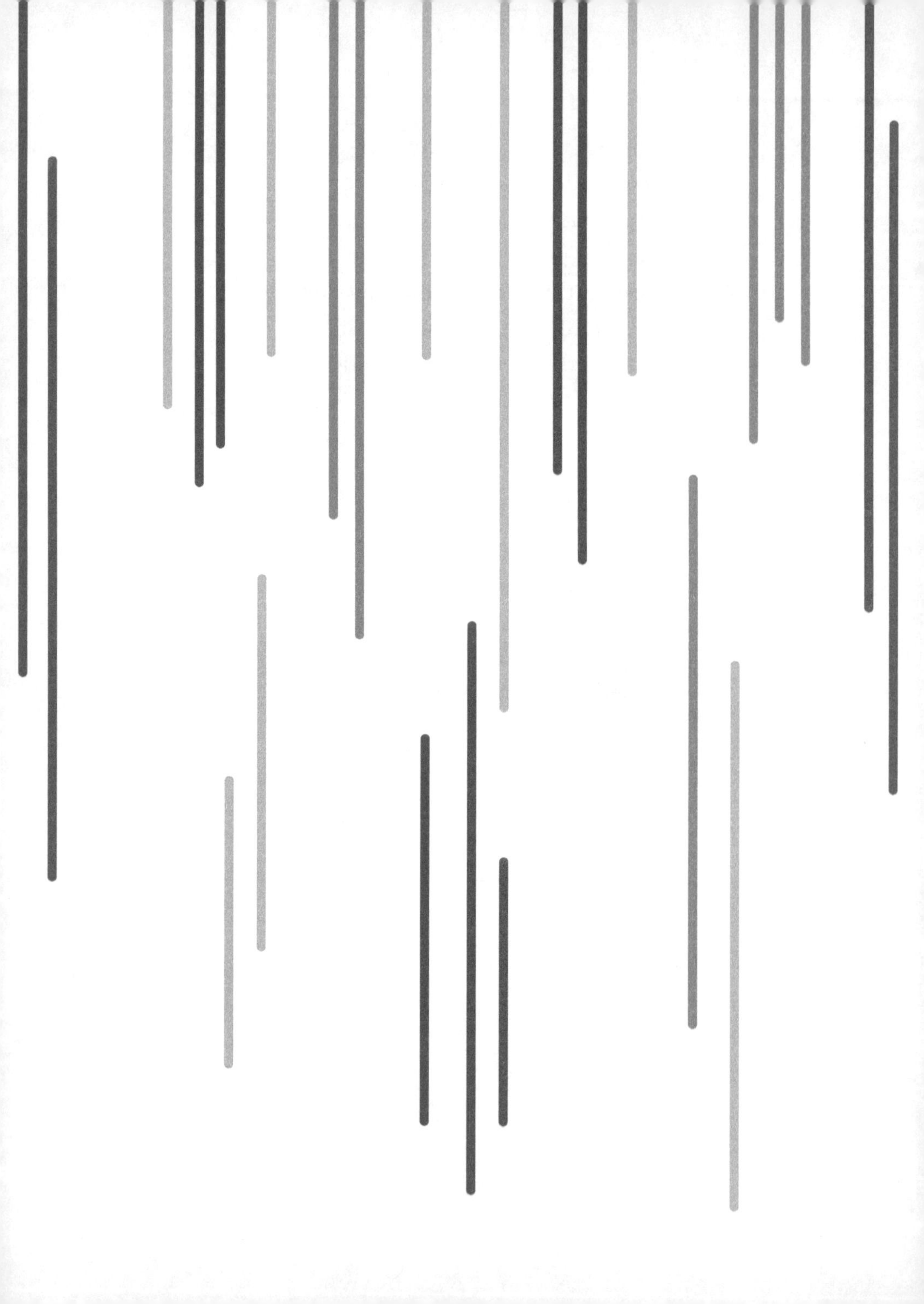

Tonight you are barefoot in LA, and you hope you are dreaming. You hope you are dreaming because you are naked and nobody is stopping to look at you. You hope you are dreaming because you can't feel your skin melting on the asphalt. You are trying so hard to say something to anyone. You are trying. You are burning. You are balanced impossibly on your own ankle bones, no one stopping to steady you. You almost thank God when you realize they all have no eyes. When you wake, because surely you'll wake, you'll have no legs at all, and people will see you. When you wake, because surely you'll wake, they'll all look, and they'll help this time. This time they'll help. This time they'll. Please. Please wake up.

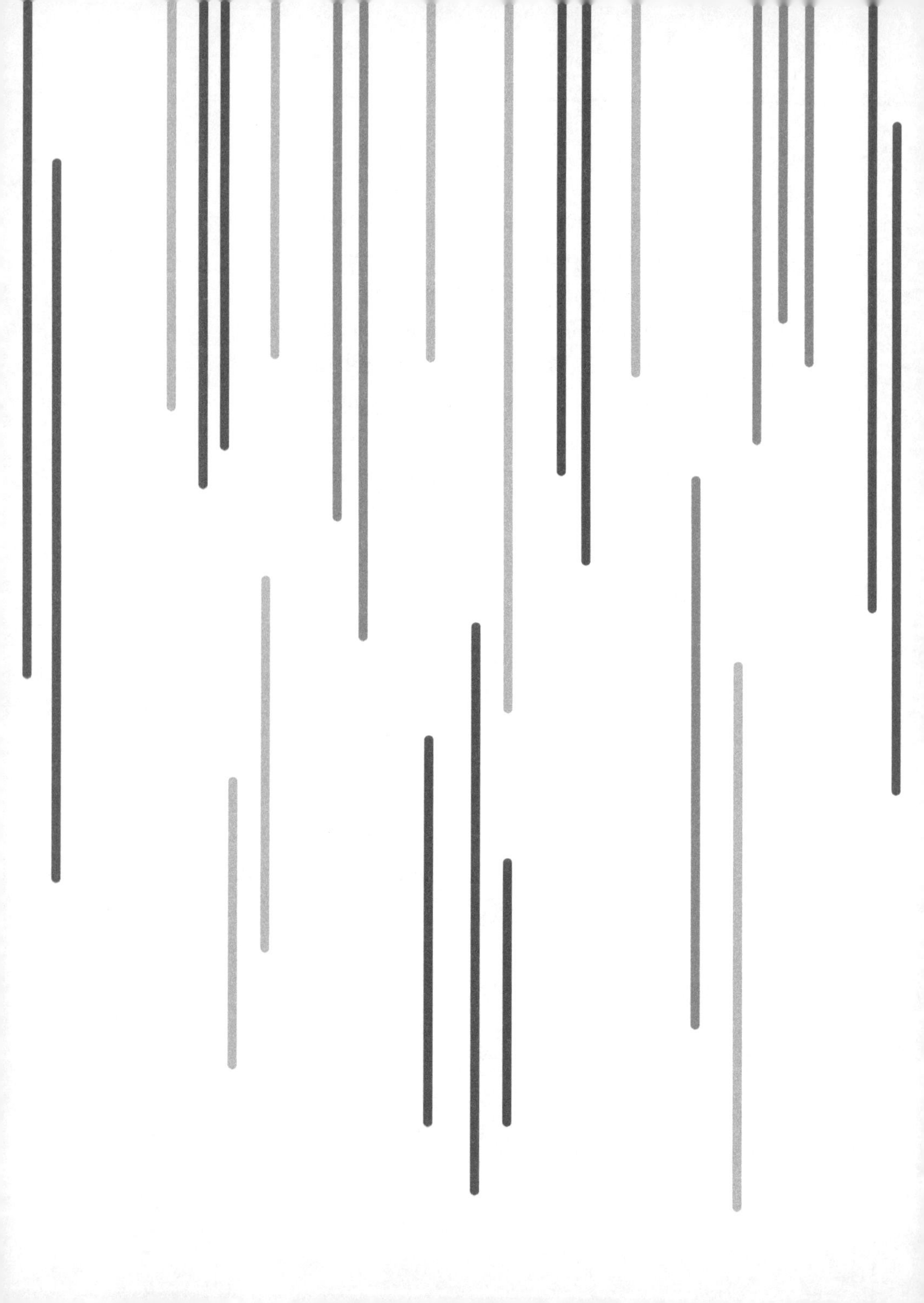

Tonight you find the devil at the bottom of a glass. He's red as Georgia dirt, says to call him Johnny. Says to call him Lucy. Says you can call him what you like; he knows it's been a hell of a day. Says they're all like that, and wouldn't he know. Says you can tell him anything, anything at all. He's not here to judge. That boss you quietly wish would up and die? Can't grant that wish, but he'll hear you out. That ex who ran off with the trucker? No, no, he's looking out for her, too, but you can call her anything you like, and he's like to agree. That dadgum senator from whatsitcalled? Oh, the stories he can't tell you about that one, but feel free to speculate. And ain't this what you were afraid of all along? Is it worse that you were right after all, that the devil don't pick sides, that he don't tell you to do nothing you don't want anyway, that his voice just goes down smooth like the. Like the. Like whichever bottle that was. The house. It's a bottle. You're a fly. There's no spider.

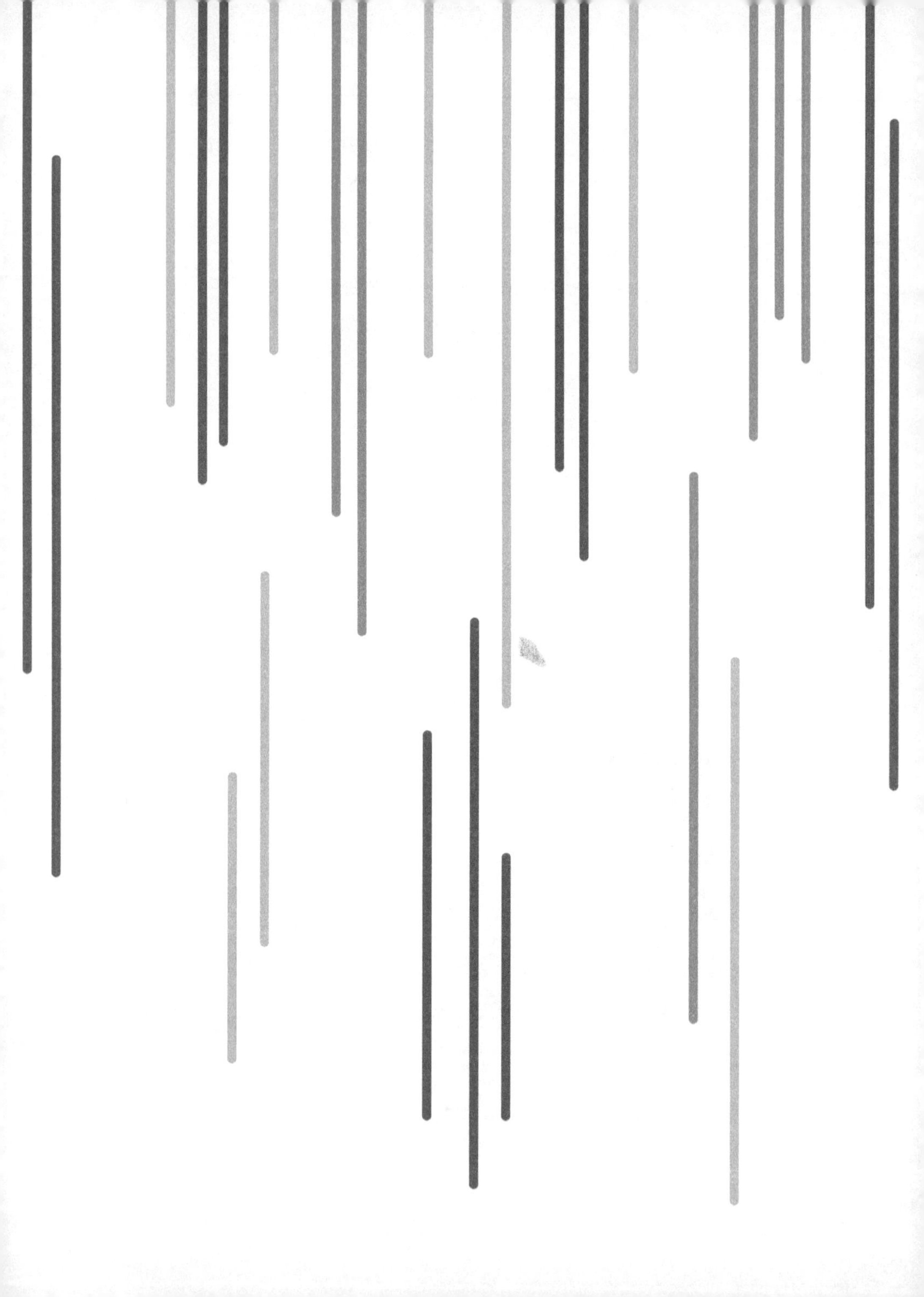

Tonight you have mushrooms growing in your lungs. Or blood in your gut. *I swallowed a scalpel*, you tell the doctor, and you can feel it knocking against rocks. The doctor smiles, says, *Everything will be okay.* The doctor in his bright white lab coat opens the door, and two more men in bright white lab coats come in and put a hand on each of your shoulders. They put a bright white lab coat on you, but it's a trick, you see, because it turns into a straightjacket. The men and the doctor are in their straightjackets, and they laugh and laugh, and you laugh, too. *I'm cured*, you call out, *I can go home now.* Everything is bright and funny. The nurse in her bright white lab coat closes the door, says, *Goodnight.* Through the small window, it almost sounds like *we're all in here together.*

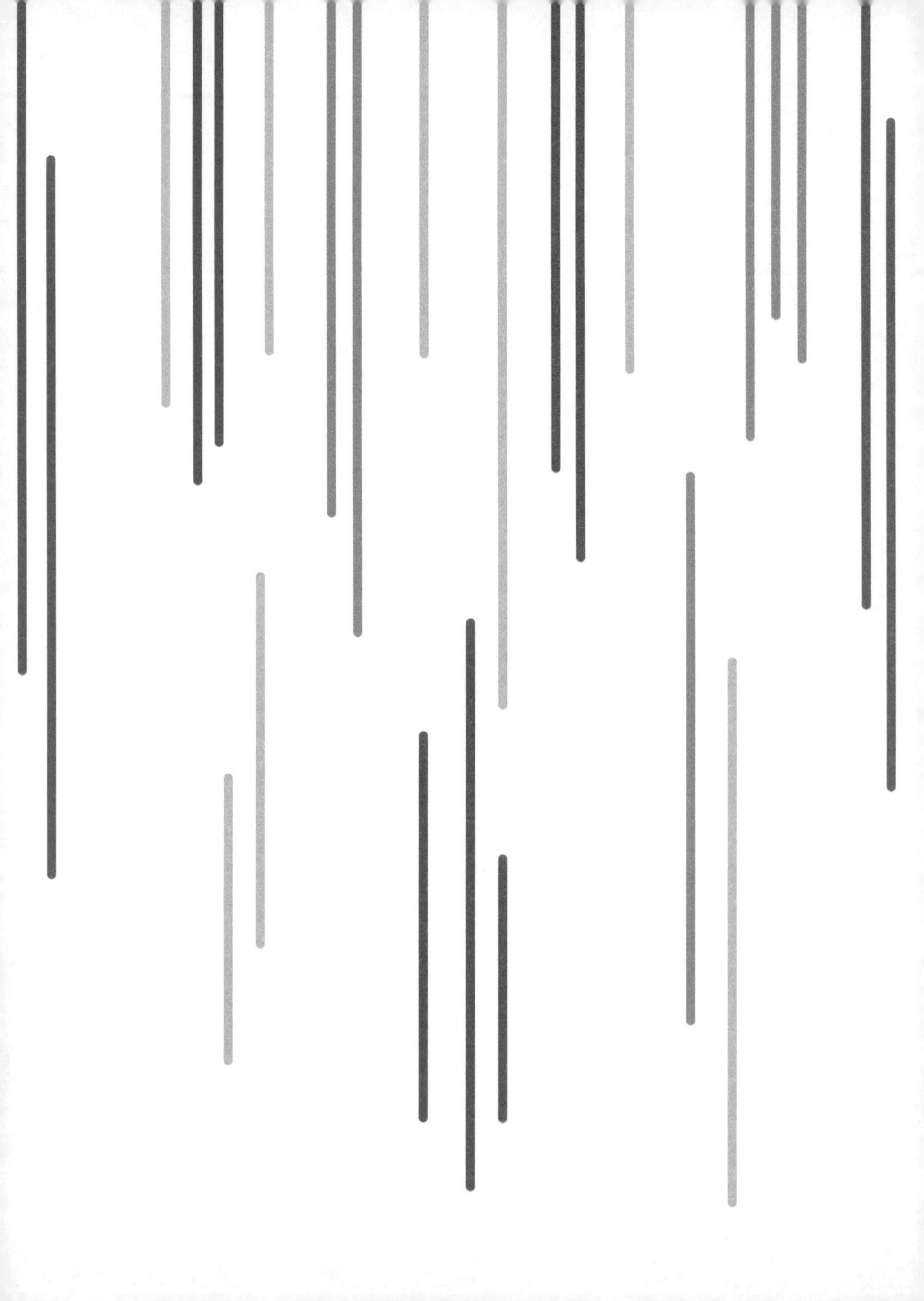

Tonight you are in an antique factory, watching watches and fine china roll down conveyer belts. They pass through some kind of machine and come out dusty and crackled. You see a grandfather clock compressed as in a cartoon and emerge with an off-key chime, see a chest of drawers gain a water-stained patina. You watch for what seems like forever. A tour group comes walking through, asks you questions like you work there. You don't, of course, but you know all the answers anyway. You've observed for ages. You've lived in the factory as long as you can recall. A cracked mirror pops out, and you catch a glimpse of yourself. You are old, creased. You are valuable and valued, at least to the people walking through. The group moves on to make room for the next, the tour guide naming things as they do: *mirror, dresser, watch, survivor.*

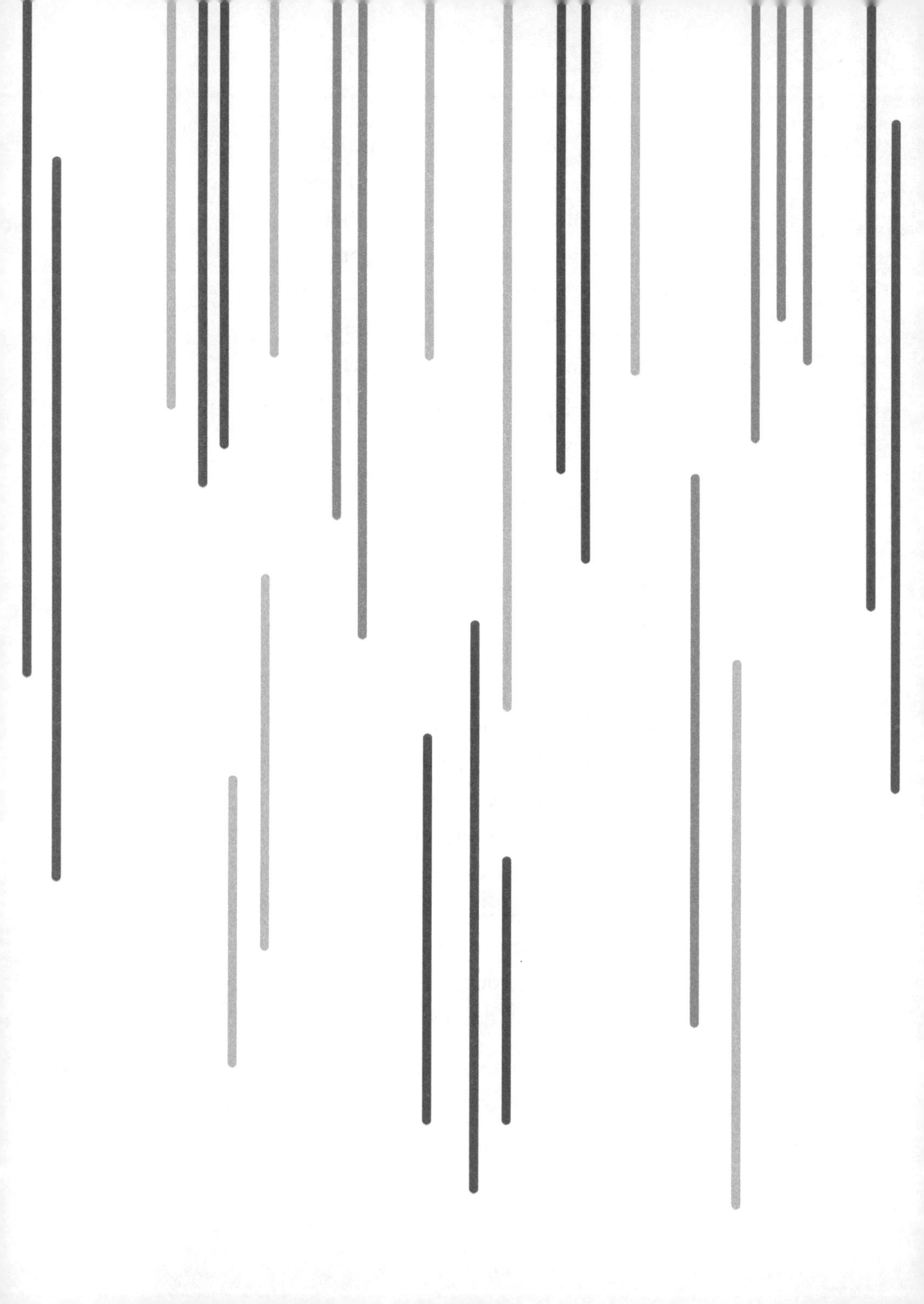

Tonight you are in the right body. You know this because your mind is quiet. It's peaceful here. The Earth is not trying to draw you into itself. You are not a dinosaur bone abject among the rocks. There's a muffled thought somewhere, that you expected this moment would be all action, but instead it is defined by absence - no judge and no jury, no pebble lodged where it doesn't belong. You recall being Sisyphus. You recall the condemnation. But now. Now you are free. There is a stone rolling down a hill, and you are walking the other way. There once was a god who said to you, *Forever*, but that isn't your name anymore.

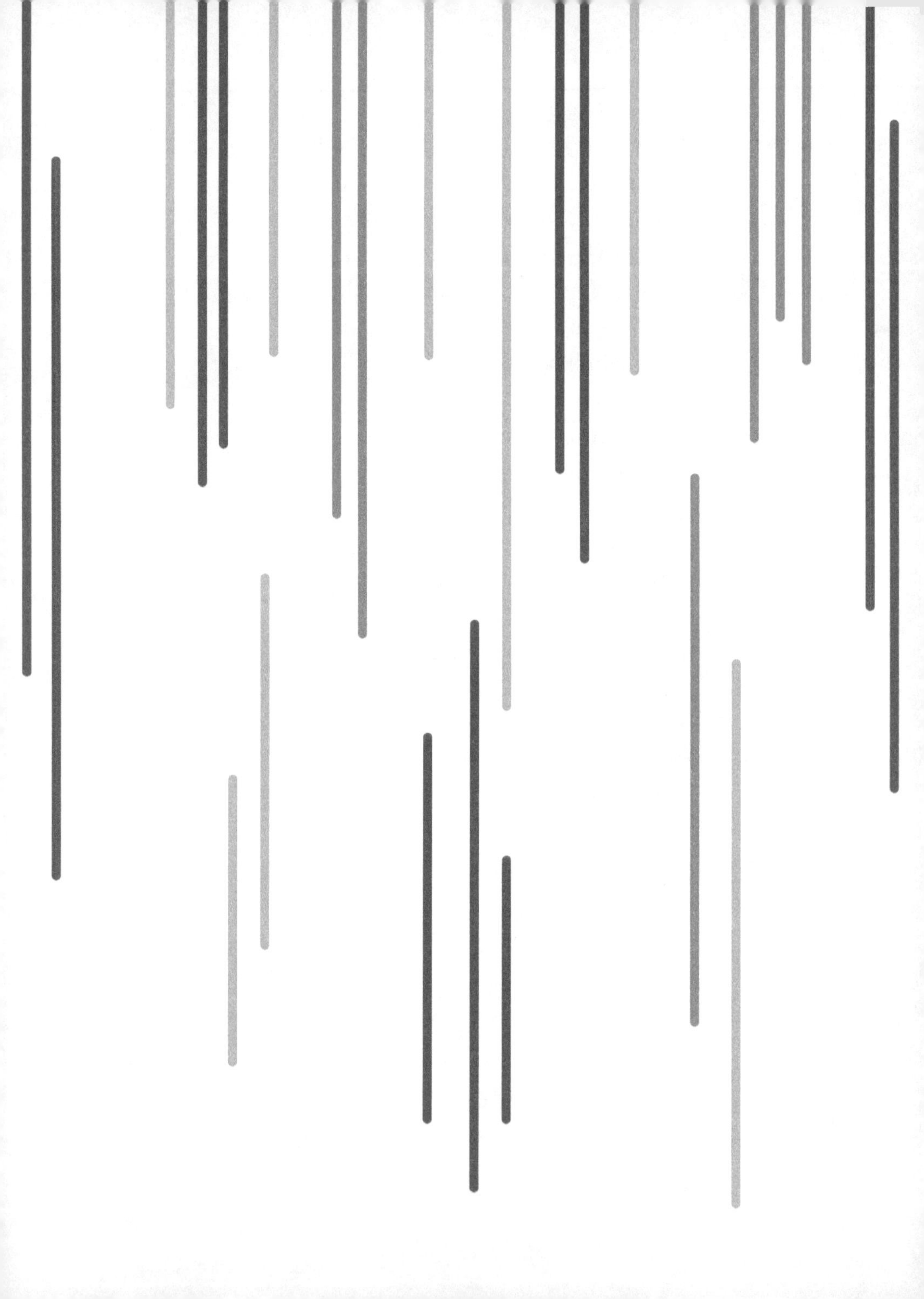

acknowledgments

2River: [Tonight you are barefoot in LA...], [Tonight you are a confused werewolf howling at the sun...], [Tonight you are building something...], [Tonight you are bound in the backwoods...]

DMQ Review: [Tonight you are bagging groceries...]

For You: [Tonight you are in the right body...]

Gulf Stream Magazine: [Tonight you are an insect bound by window-magic...]

Half and One: [Tonight you are paddling a canoe in the middle of the ocean...], [Tonight you are arguing with yourself over whether or not you can fly...]

The Journal: [Tonight you are between rows of blueberry bushes...], [Tonight you are watching the whales migrate...]

Pangyrus: [Tonight you are seated at the base of a tree in the desert...]

The Plaza Prizes Anthology 2: [Tonight you are pregnant and your fetus has a gun...]

Prairie Schooner: [Tonight you are walking in the deep woods...], [Tonight you have teeth growing out of your teeth...]

The Quarter(ly): [Tonight you are a security camera panning across a small room...]

Salt Hill Journal: [Tonight you are plowing through clouds of locusts on a motorcycle...], [Tonight you are at Times Square or possibly the end of the world...], [Tonight you are a watch face spinning like a gyroscope...],

[Tonight you are seated in a darkened tent…], [Tonight you are the echo in the bottom of the well…]

Subnivean: [Tonight you are wascally…], [Tonight you are tusked…], [Tonight you are caught in a strobe-light childhood…], [Tonight you are looking at a beautiful woman…]

Unbroken: [Tonight you are a heart attack on stilettos…]

Voicemail Poems: [Tonight you lie on your own couch…]

The poems published in *Subnivean* are part of a group of poems that won the 2024 Subnivean Award in Poetry, judged by Major Jackson. [Tonight you are pregnant and your fetus has a gun…] was shortlisted for the 2023 Plaza Prose Poetry Prize. *DMQ Review* nominated [Tonight you are bagging groceries…] for a Pushcart Prize.

In the poem [Tonight you are at Times Square or possibly the end of the world…], the closing quotation, "Earth is calling in her little ones, '*Come home, come home*'," is from "They Feed They Lion" by Philip Levine.

notes and appreciation

In 2017, after I ended up in the ER with stroke-like symptoms, the attending neurologist asked me about my sleep. I told him I had violent nightmares every night that left me waking up more tired than when I'd gone to bed, and he told me that's not how it is for most people. I had up to that moment perhaps become complacent. In 2009, when I was twenty-nine, I had my second psychotic break, only this time it got diagnosed properly, and I started on an antipsychotic. The world grew still. I didn't feel or see things that weren't there in my waking hours. And I thought that the fact that my nights were still haunted was good enough to get by. It obviously wasn't.

I finished, barely, the semester I was teaching. Tried and failed to hold down a couple of part-time jobs. Ended up on disability. And I stopped writing for five years.

In 2022, I wrote around 120 prose poems that began as a self-driven therapy exercise: Take my dreams and externalize them so that they could be treated as something other than, well, me. But, as I've taught, what is therapeutic for the writer is not necessarily meaningful, let alone cathartic, for the reader, and so I looked for lessons in some of those dreams and began to write in epiphanies that I'd been too tired or too terrified to grapple with in the moment. About halfway through the process, I was listening to the hopes and fears of people I knew and turning them into dreamscapes. The result, completed around the end of that year, was a mass of "nightmares" with occasional breakthroughs of positivity. It wasn't just me, and it wasn't just for me.

Thank you to everyone who read drafts of these poems and especially for making sure I was rendering truths when writing experiences outside of my own. To Angelo & Darrell & Dawn & Ellen & Emilia & James & Lisa & Morgan & also the handful of people I showed a single poem to and you just went, "Yeah, that's messed up," and meant it as a compliment. Thank you to Kate for sticking by me despite decades of thrashing in my sleep. Thank you to risperidone for taking away these moments in my waking hours and to prazosin and cannabis for sometimes managing to stop them at night. Thank you to Diannely Antigua for selecting this manuscript for the Granite State Poetry Prize and to the readers at Yas Press for advancing it to her and to Danielle Jones at Yas for ushering it into print.

THE NOSSRAT YASSINI POETRY FESTIVAL at UNH celebrates the power of poetry to unify, bring people together, and build a better community. Poetry is the oldest literary art form and the one we turn to in times of great joy, sorrow, and inspiration. Because we treasure and remember the poems that have influenced our lives, celebrating poetry can bring us together in uniquely powerful ways. This world class festival brings together poets, students, teachers, and poetry lovers of all kinds to experience the poetic richness of New Hampshire and the New England community.

YAS PRESS, housed in the University of New Hampshire's English department, publishes three books a year featuring the best poetry in New Hampshire: an anthology of teen poetry, an anthology of USNH student poetry, and a previously unpublished poetry collection of extraordinary quality written by an emerging or established New Hampshire poet. These prize-winning publications are made possible through the generous support of the YAS Foundation in honor of poet and poetry lover, Nossrat Yassini. In addition, The Nossrat Yassini Poetry Prize—an annual award given each year to a first book published by a U.S. poet of extraordinary promise—is managed by the Press.

JeFF Stumpo is the author of five chap-
books of poetry (most through Seven Kitch-
ens Press), a survivor of psychosis and PTSD,
husband to a PhD chemist, and father to an
amazing trans son. You can find his literary
updates at www.JeFFStumpo.com.